Iberia and Latin America

Iberia and Latin America

New Democracies, New Policies, New Models

Howard J. Wiarda

ROWMAN & LITTLEFIELD PUBLISHERS, INC.

ROWMAN & LITTLEFIELD PUBLISHERS, INC.

Published in the United States of America
by Rowman & Littlefield Publishers, Inc.
4720 Boston Way, Lanham, Maryland 20706

3 Henrietta Street
London WC2E 8LU, England

Copyright © 1996 by Rowman & Littlefield Publishers, Inc.

British Cataloging in Publication Information Available

Library of Congress Cataloging-in-Publication Data

Wiarda, Howard J.,
Iberia and Latin America : new democracies, new policies, new
models / Howard J. Wiarda.
p.   cm.
Includes bibliographical references and index.
1. Democracy—Spain.   2. Democracy—Portugal.   3. Democracy—Latin
America.   4. Spain—Politics and government—1975-   5. Portugal—
Politics and government—1974-   6. Latin America—Politics and
government—1980-   I. Title.
JN8341.W52   1996   320.917′561—dc20   96–13821   CIP

ISBN 0–8476–8252–8 (cloth : alk. paper)
ISBN 0–8476–8253–6 (pbk. : alk. paper)

Printed in the United States of America

♾™ The paper used in this publication meets the minimum requirements of
American National Standard for Information Sciences—Permanence of
Paper for Printed Library Materials, ANSI Z39.48–1984.

Contents

Preface

Over the last thirty-five years my research and scholarship have focused on two main areas: Latin America and Iberia. I began life, academically that is, during the 1960s as a Latin Americanist.[1] But the more I studied Latin America, the more I became convinced that to understand the region fully I needed to go back and understand its colonial, medieval, and quasi-feudal origins in Spain and Portugal. So I spent much of the 1970s doing research and writing about Portugal and Spain,[2] as well as what came to be called the Iberic-Latin "corporatist model" of development.[3] During the 1980s I continued to write about both Iberia and Latin America, as well as the complex interrelations between them.[4]

In the course of this considerable research sojourn, I have noticed that while my writings on Latin America are well known by Latin Americanists, they are almost completely unknown by those who study Spain and Portugal. Similarly, while my writings on Iberia are known by scholars of Spain and Portugal, they are almost entirely unknown by those who study Latin America. This is a curious phenomenon. Despite the fact that scholars in both areas are dedicated to the study of *comparative* sociology and *comparative* politics, the realities of geographic separation and academic specialization mean that there is seldom much cross-fertilization and mutual scholarly enrichment between students of the two areas.

This omission is particularly glaring given their shared histories during the colonial period and the vastly increased international relations—cultural, political, economic, diplomatic—between Iberia and Latin America in the last two decades (which also, for both areas, often involves an even more complex *trilateral* relationship with the United States). But more than that, in the literature on corporatism, on organic-statism, and on transitions to democracy—three of the most important approaches in the comparative politics field—a number of us have also tried to argue that there are common

vii

themes and approaches, parallel patterns, and even a common intellectual framework and model that can be used for the study of both Iberia and Latin America. For it is not just by history and recent foreign relations that Iberia and Latin America are linked but also, deeply and fundamentally, by languages, shared sociology, political culture, legal system, religion, intellectual origins, and politics and economics. An approach that intimately links Iberia and Latin America and uses a common model for both areas, however, is often very controversial, not only because of the physical and geographic separation between the two areas and the financial and scholarly difficulties of doing research in both regions; but also because Latin America is not always convinced that it must follow the Spanish/Portuguese lead, while Spaniards and Portuguese (and the scholars who study these two countries)—now oriented toward Europe—are not at all sure they wish to be considered in the same categories as Latin America.

These complex and often convoluted relationships, which involve not just the relations between nations and areas but their cultural, intellectual, and scholarly relations as well, are the subject of this book—and of its companion volume published also by Rowman & Littlefield.[5] In these books we focus on Latin America, Iberia, and their common background, the growing relations between these two areas, and the relations of both of them to the United States. Our focus throughout is on political culture, social and political change, and public policy-making in both the domestic and the international terrains. Our goal is not only to understand Spain, Portugal, and Latin America better but also to analyze common cultural currents, parallel as well as contrasting patterns of development, and perhaps, in exploratory fashion, to set forth a common model of sociopolitical change.

In the original plan for the book, Latin America was to receive most of the attention, with a subsection included on Iberia. That chapter outline was long and unwieldy so the publisher suggested the project be divided into two volumes: one on Latin America and one on Iberia. That stroke of genius on the publisher's part enables us to provide in the two volumes the detail and nuance that would not have been possible had we been forced to include all the material in a single, shortened volume.

The volume on Latin America, already published, thus focuses on the policy processes, the transitions to democracy, various case studies, and the fashioning of a model of Latin American development. The present, complementary volume concentrates on the political transformations in Spain and Portugal, on Iberian–Latin American relations, on assessing the strength of democratic institutions in both areas, and on developing a common intellectual framework for assessing change.

Several of the chapters included here were published previously in preliminary form, but often in foreign journals or in hard-to-find or out-of-print volumes. They have been lightly edited to bring them up to date or to reflect revised interpretations. These chapters help provide the substance on which the far-reaching interpretations found in the Introduction and Conclusion are based. The book and the ideas it and the companion volume on Latin America contain may be of special interest to students and scholars of Iberia, Latin America, comparative models of development, and international relations. The two books may be used together or separately in courses and seminars on Latin America, Iberia, Comparative Politics, International Relations, and Foreign Policy.

In the course of preparing these volumes and the ongoing *ouvre* of which they are part, many debts have been incurred. Institutional support came from the Center for International Affairs at Harvard University; the Department of Political Science at the University of Massachusetts/Amherst; the Center for Strategic and International Studies in Washington, D.C.; and the National War College, part of the National Defense University, also in Washington. Financial support came from the Tinker Foundation, the Fulbright Program, and the United States Institute of Peace. Doris Holden did her usual superb and very professional preparation of the manuscript. Useful comments on parts or all of the manuscript were offered by Peter Hakim, Michael J. Kryzanek, Edward Mariscioulo, Viron P. Vaky, Iêda Siqueira Wiarda, and Larman C. Wilson. None of these institutions or individuals is responsible for the views expressed, however, nor do the opinions stated represent the official positions of the institutions listed. Only the author bears responsibility for the entire project.

Howard J. Wiarda
Commuting (as usual) among
Amherst, Cambridge, and Washington, D.C.

Notes

1. My early writings were concentrated on the Dominican Republic and Brazil: see *Dictatorship and Development: The Methods of Control in Trujillo's Dominican Republic* (Gainesville: University of Florida Press, 1968); *The Dominican Republic: Nation in Transition* (New York: Praeger, 1969); *The Brazilian Catholic Labor Movement: The Dilemmas of National Development* (Amherst: University of Massachusetts, Labor Relations and Research Center, 1969); *Dictatorship, Development, and Disintegration: Politics and Social Change in the Dominican Republic* (Ann Arbor: Monograph Series, Xerox University Microfilms, 3 vols., 1975).

2. *Corporatism and Development: The Portuguese Experience* (Amherst: University

of Massachusetts Press, 1977); *Transcending Corporatism? The Portuguese Corporative System and the Revolution of 1974* (Columbia: University of South Carolina, Institute of International Studies, 1976); *The Transition to Democracy in Spain and Portugal* (Washington, D.C.: The American Enterprise Institute for Public Policy Research, 1987); and *Politics in Iberia: The Political Systems of Spain and Portugal* (New York: Harper Collins, 1992).

3. "Toward a Framework for the Study of Political Change in the Iberic-Latin Tradition," *World Politics* 26 (January 1973), 206–35; *Politics and Social Change in Latin America*, 3rd ed. (Boulder, Colo.: Westview Press, 1992); *Corporatism and National Development in Latin America* (Boulder, Colo.: Westview, 1981).

4. *The Iberian–Latin American Connection: Implications for U.S. Foreign Policy* (Boulder, Colo.: Westview, 1986).

5. *Democracy and Its Discontents: Development, Interdependence and U.S. Policy in Latin America* (Lanham, Md.: Rowman & Littlefield, 1995).

Chapter 1

Introduction: A New Spain, A New Portugal?—And the Latin American Connection

Within my academic lifetime (so far!)—from the late-1950s through the mid-1990s—Iberia and Latin America have been profoundly transformed. Countries that were 70 percent rural and 70 percent illiterate are now 70 percent urban and 70 percent literate. Countries that were "sleepy," "backward," and "underdeveloped" are now rushing pell-mell toward modernity—or are already there! Countries that were economically autarchic, mercantilist, and a part of the Third World have seen, in many cases, their levels of per capita income double and then double again within a thirty-year period, while also opening up to free trade and global competition. And along with these vast socioeconomic changes have come greater political pluralism, mobilization, and democratization. It is often hard to imagine that Iberia and Latin America could change so much within such a short period of time—literally, one generation; my generation![1]

While the changes have no doubt been impressive and are even measurable using standard indicators, the deeper question of what all these changes *mean* for Iberia and Latin America—and how we interpret these changes—remains very much alive as well as controversial. Have Iberia and Latin America now, finally, left feudalism and the Middle Ages behind? Do vast socioeconomic change and mobilization inevitably translate into stabler and more democratic political systems? Have these two areas now, definitively, left in the past the Third World of underdeveloped nations and joined the First World of modern industrial nations? Does the growth of a middle class in Iberia and Latin America mean that this new middle class will also share the assumed middle-class virtues of stability, moderation, and adherence to democracy and human rights? Have trade unions in Iberia and Latin America become less politicized, more moderate, and inclined toward collective bargaining? Have the armed forces become more professionalized (by our lights) and more inclined to accept unquestioned civilian control? In short, while the socioeconomic changes over the past forty years have been exceedingly impressive, have the political changes that are supposed to follow upon or occur concomitant with these changes been equally thoroughgoing? Though many institutional structures (parties, elections, parliaments, etc.) have evolved in the direction of democracy, how much has the underlying political culture also become egalitarian and democratic? For while it is relatively easy to change institutions, we all understand that it is far harder to change underlying culture and behavior.

These questions—the relations between socioeconomic modernization on the one hand and political democratization on the other, between institutional change at one level and more basic political-cultural transformations at another, and therefore what model or models (corporatist, organic-statist, liberal, or democratic are among the candidates) to use to interpret Iberia and Latin America—are at the core of the analysis in this book. We raise these questions in the Introduction, explore them in the body of the volume, and then try to offer assessments—doubtless provocative and controversial—in the Conclusion. Specifically, the Introduction raises the following main themes explored in order in the chapter's main subsections: the transitions to democracy in Iberia and Latin America, the degree to which these have become consolidated and institutionalized, how much has *really* changed in these societies, the common as well as conflicting trends in Iberia and Latin America as well as their complex international relations, whether and to what extent we can use a common culture-area approach to understanding these two areas, and whether there is a single and shared Iberic-Latin model of development. The issues are complex and the answers open to great dispute.

Transitions to Democracy

During the past two decades the world has seen some remarkable transitions to democracy. Beginning with Portugal, Greece, and Spain in the mid-1970s, the democratic wave has swept over most of Latin America, strongly influenced Asia, helped to recast Russia and Eastern Europe, and impacted Africa and the Islamic world.[2] The emergence of democracy in so many areas of the globe is surely one of the great epochal transformations of the last quarter of the twentieth century, and rivals for importance and often runs parallel to the dissolution of communism, the fall of the Berlin Wall, and the collapse of the Soviet Union and the Warsaw Pact.

Although pundits have often derided his book seemingly without having read or understood it, Francis Fukuyama's thesis about the triumph of democracy signaling the "end of history" appears to have been vindicated.[3] By the use of that phrase Fukuyama did not have in mind some superficial notion that all history has stopped; rather he meant that in the Hegelian sense of the dialectical march of *ideas* in history, the democratic idea has definitively triumphed. Surely one would be hard pressed currently to conceive of any other idea and *system* of politics now or in the immediate future rivaling the legitimacy that democracy now enjoys: not communism, not fascism, not Marxism, not authoritarianism, not corporatism, or any other "ism" that the modern world has thrown at us. Although democracy may take many different forms and though there may still be distinctive definitions of democracy (one of the main themes of this book), and though obviously *history* writ large (ethnic strife, racial turmoil, the conflicting pursuit of different national interests, many other issues) will continue, the democratic *idea* does seem clearly to have triumphed at least as far into the future as it is possible to foresee.

Spain, Portugal, and Latin America have been in the forefront of these democratic transitions and have even been put forth as models for other countries to emulate. Surely the record in both Iberia and Latin America has been impressive: regular and fair elections, for the most part, in both areas, competitive party politics, more pluralist interest groups, peaceful transitions from one elected administration to the next, more effective and responsible public policies, and vastly improved situations of human rights. Spain and Portugal appear to be safely in the democratic camp; in Latin America nineteen out of twenty countries—all except Cuba—live under regimes that could be called democratic.

It is surely accurate to say that these countries have successfully completed a *transition* to democracy—although in some of the less institutionalized countries the transition is still shaky and incomplete. Nevertheless at this stage we can pretty well say the initial transitions are complete; what now remains to be done is the *consolidation* of democracy. But in this second phase many problems and questions remain; among them (and discussed more fully in the body of the book) are:

1. There remain pockets of resistance to democracy, groups who still years afterward have not yet reconciled themselves to democracy. These groups are, in general, not strong enough any more in most countries to overthrow democracy, but antidemocratic groups are still stronger in Spain, Portugal,

and Latin America than in more established democracies and they can still cause many and severe problems.

2. Democracy has proved disappointing to many people in these countries and has not delivered on its promises. The euphoria present in the early years of the democratic transitions has worn off; disillusionment has often set in. In many cases, standards of living and social and economic advancement and opportunities have not grown rapidly enough to satisfy the new expectations that have been raised; in other cases the new wealth created has been poorly distributed; in still others the economic indicators have gone down, adding to the disillusionment.

3. Iberia's and Latin America's *forms* and *meanings* of democracy are often at variance from our own. Democracy in these areas tends to be more centralized, organic, unified, statist, Rousseauian, and corporatist than would be permissible in the United States.[4] Such diversity of meanings may be a good and healthy sign; but then again, it may not. At the least, the issue needs to be kept open and investigated, not brushed over or swept under the rug.

4. Spain and Portugal (the main focus of this volume) have now reached a living standard about 60–65 percent that of most of the rest of Western Europe; indices of literacy and other social indicators are similarly about two-thirds the European level.[5] But if Spain and Portugal are only two-thirds European, they are one-third something else. What is the other one-third? Could it be Spain and Portugal are two-thirds European and still one-third Latin American? Or Third World? Therein lies a major controversy. And what are the implications of such a reading?

5. If Spain and Portugal, by most indices of modernization, are only two-thirds of the way to reaching European standards, it implies that this transition—and to democracy as well—is incomplete, a continuum and an ongoing process rather than an either-or proposition. All democracies, after all, remain incomplete in some particulars. But if this is true, is it not therefore false and misleading for us to say that Spain and Portugal have *finalized* the transition to democracy or that they are "safely in the democratic camp"? They are—and they *may* not be. The issue is one of degrees rather than an absolute "yes" or "no." We need, therefore, to measure these degrees and the processes involved with precision. Wishful thinking and wishful political sociology need to be avoided. Are Spain and Portugal as democratic as Switzerland? As Holland, Sweden, or Austria? More democratic than Argentina and Chile and by what criteria? Clearly if we consider democratic regimes on a continuum from strongly democratic to weakly democratic, rather than the simplistic issue of yes or no, we introduce a host of issues and uncertainties into the equation that must be taken into account.

Change versus Continuity

It is obvious to everyone that a great deal has changed in Iberia since the Portuguese revolution of 1974 and the death of Franco in 1975. Persons who knew Spain and Portugal in the 1960s and early 1970s would hardly recognize these two countries today. The authoritarian structures of the old regime came tumbling down; democracy has been established. A consumer-oriented society has replaced the austerity of the past. Catholicism and the older values have in large part been rejected in favor of a new emphasis on freedom and liberty. Teenagers go on dates without chaperones, the sexual revolution has come to Spain and Portugal, and divorce is prevalent. Young people often live together without marrying and the pornography is as graphic and readily available as any in Europe—although, significantly, few Spaniards like or buy it. They want the freedom, long denied by Franco, to be *able* to buy it but that is not to say they like it or the degradation of women that it portrays.

While Spain and Portugal have changed dramatically over the past twenty years, there are important continuities as well—and these have received far less attention. Moreover, the areas of national life exhibiting important continuities are quite fundamental ones. For example, while the Spanish and Portuguese states have changed from authoritarian to democratic over the course of the past two decades, the leading, guiding, and directing role of the state in many areas of political, economic, and social life remains clear. No Spaniard or Portuguese would ever make the mistake, as American political science often did under the theory of interest group liberalism, of thinking of the state as purely a neutral referee among interest groups, an umpire who does not himself get involved in the struggle. Instead, the state in Iberia remains a *dirigiste* state, a strong state, often (we have recently seen) a corrupt and patrimonialist state. Spain and Portugal are not *laissez-faire* states, there has been (unlike Latin America) limited downsizing or privatizing of the state (EEC subsidies have enabled Spain and Portugal to avoid such painful adjustments), and the state still regulates—often heavy-handedly—vast areas of national socioeconomic life. What has been called the "neoliberal revolution" of deregulation and free markets has so far barely begun to have an impact on Spain and Portugal where statism still reigns supreme.[6]

A second area of continuity lies in the relations of the state to interest groups. Under Franco and Portugal's Salazar—and for an even longer time historically—these relations were governed by top-down, state authority (called "corporatism") in which the state licensed, regulated, controlled, and generally monopolized the group life that swirled about it. Since the end of the old dictatorships, interest group activity has become considerably freer; nevertheless, the licensing, regulating, controlling, and monopolizing functions have often been maintained albeit in new forms. For example, it is still far harder in Spain and Portugal to organize an interest group than it is in the United States; in Iberia interest groups are still limited in number, they must still be accepted and licensed by the state, and in order for them to participate legitimately in the political process their "juridical personality" must be recognized (which also carries with it the power *not* to recognize). Moreover, the succession of "social pacts" agreed to by labor and business under state direction and sometimes duress bear a striking resemblance to the corporatism of the old regimes—*neo*corporatism perhaps, but still corporatism.

A third area requiring further analysis is in the area of values or political culture. We all know that Iberian values and political culture have changed dramatically in recent decades, but are there continuities here as well? For example, while certain key democratic political values seem to be solidly enshrined in both Spain and Portugal (support of elections and democratic functions, for instance), social and class values and attitudes appear to have changed far less dramatically. Class lines are still often sharply drawn in both countries (far more so than in the United States or the north of Europe), class consciousness is omnipresent, and elite attitudes often prevail. These include, oftentimes, disdain for manual labor *and* for those who engage in it, haughty and aristocratic attitudes toward those lower in the social scale, an exaggerated sense of self-importance and of social hierarchy, and condescending and patronizing attitudes and behavior to those who fall below one's own rank. To these features we must now add widespread corruption, patrimonialism, family and clan favoritism, and a blurring of the lines between public and private. Many of these are the traits of an earlier and traditional society; to the extent they remain prevalent in Spain and Portugal they do not augur well for democracy.

Iberia and Latin America

Like the relations between all former colonies and their former mother countries, the relations between Latin America and Spain and Portugal are very complicated. They are infused with deeply emotional sentiments as well as neutral and more rational calculations of national interest. At times, Latin America has admired and felt close to the mother countries, at other times it has loathed the former colonial powers. The relationship is in some ways akin to that governing U.S.–Latin American relations: a complex, love-hate relationship that not only varies over time but also varies within countries and individuals whose attitudes may encompass love and hate at the same time.

For over three hundred years (approximately 1500–1800) Latin America was subject to Spanish and Portuguese colonial administration. The colonial countries brought law, language, religion, culture, education, social and political structure, and Western civilization (albeit the civilization of the counter-reformation, of scholasticism, of Hapsburg absolutism, of premodern Europe) to the New World. At the same time they brought bloody conquest, sickness and disease, rigid and authoritarian rule, slavery and feudalism, closed and absolutist religious and educational institutions, the suppression of indigenous societies and cultures, mercantilism and an exploitive economic system, and an unyielding social structure based on both class and race. Given this mixed legacy, it should not be surprising that Latin America's attitudes toward the mother countries encompass both love and hate.

After independence in the 1820s, hate dominated. For a long time in the nineteenth century Latin America continued to resent the two mother countries of Spain and Portugal. They were blamed for imposing a religious orthodoxy on Latin America, for milking the colonies dry of their wealth, for authoritarian institutions and lack of preparation in self-government, and for a legacy of feudalism. Rather than admiration of the mother countries, the dominant attitude in Latin America was resentment—made worse by Spain's and Portugal's own sagging fortunes in the nineteenth century, which rendered them unable to assist their former colonies with development. But Spain's and Portugal's attitudes toward Latin America were often similarly dismissive, castigating Latin America for not being grateful for the Catholicism and civilization that the mother countries had brought them, while also speaking disparagingly of Latin America for its inability to govern itself and referring to Latin Americans using coded racial slurs as people from "the Indies." Until 1898 the post-independence relations of Iberia and Latin America were not happy.

With Spain's defeat in the Spanish-American War of 1898, Latin America's views of the former mother country became more sympathetic. Spain's weakness as revealed in the war meant that it was no longer a threat to recapture and recolonize Latin America, as many had feared in the nineteenth century; within Latin America, meanwhile, there was by now greater sympathy for things Hispanic (language, literature, religion, culture), less inclination to blame the mother countries for its problems, and greater interest in ties that bound the two areas together rather than the forces pulling them apart. Spain tried to capitalize on this new-found sympathy in Latin America by pursuing a policy of *hispanismo*, which emphasized common cultural ties between Iberia and Latin America but under Spain's leadership;

however for a long time in the nineteenth and early twentieth centuries the policy floundered due to a lack of resources in Spain and lack of interest in Latin America.[7]

Generalissimo Francisco Franco tried to expand and aggressively promote the concept of *hispanismo* to use it as a prop for his dictatorship and his foreign policy. He emphasized the traditional Spanish virtues, which, not by chance, also constituted the support system for his dictatorship: authority, discipline, hierarchy, obedience, order, organic unity, and corporatism. This message resonated in conservative elite and military circles in Latin America; but few bought into it, others resented Spain's efforts to try to preach to and lead the nations of Latin America, and in any case Spain still lacked the resources to implement the policy aggressively. Meanwhile, in Spain itself, the internal political culture had begun to turn away from the traditional and Francoist values, and toward Europe, democracy, and freedom.

In the post-Franco era Spain sought to turn the concept of *hispanismo* in new directions. Still using the concept as an instrument of foreign policy, Spain now sought to emphasize the values of democracy, human rights, and social justice, and to offer Spain as a model and leader for same. But while Latin America admired Spain's democratic accomplishments, it continued often to resent its efforts at leadership, to serve as tutors to Latin America (with all the condescending and paternalistic attitudes implied therein), and to serve as a "bridge" to the European Community (with whom Latin America was perfectly capable of dealing on its own, thank you). Nevertheless after Franco's death Spain followed a more aggressive foreign policy in Latin America, expanded its contacts and investments there, and attempted to put some flesh on its newly rechristened *hispanismo* policy for the first time.[8]

That brings us up to the present—and raises a variety of questions for our analysis. How successful has the new policy been? How close or extensive are the ties between Iberia and Latin America? Is Spain trying to supplant the United States as the major outside power in Latin America? What is the current attitude of Latin America toward the former mother countries? Will their foreign policies be oriented now mainly toward Europe, the United States, the Third World, or somewhere else? And, as we explore in the next section, will the new ties between Iberia and Latin America also give rise to a new, common, culture-area approach to studying and understanding these two areas?

An Iberic–Latin American Model of Development?

From closer Iberian–Latin American interrelations and long-standing cultural, language, and other ties, it is but a short step to the idea of a common

Iberic-Latin model of development. Put another way, if Spain and Portugal are still only two-thirds European and if such countries as Argentina, Chile, or Uruguay are also mainly European in their cultures, social structures, and political institutions, then why cannot these countries all be compared using some common criteria? Why not a paradigm, especially given the shared histories and cultures of Iberia and Latin America, that combine these two *geographic* regions into a common, *culture-area* approach? Why not a common framework, a social science model that shows both the common themes and the differences between these two regions?

The answer is, there is no reason *intellectually* not to think of a common Iberic–Latin social science model. But there are a host of *political* considerations that get in the way.

Here, in essence, is the dilemma. As long as we are talking only about glorious and praiseworthy events, such as human rights accomplishments and the transition to democracy, then both Iberia and Latin America are happy to think of each other in common terms. In the case of Spain, this is especially true if Spain's role as a leader of and model for democratization in Latin America is acknowledged. But in my view, such a common Iberic-Latin model would also, in addition to democracy, have to encompass such features as patrimonialism, a heritage of elitism and authoritarianism, organic statism, and corporatism. At best, these latter are not very attractive features of the Iberic-Latin tradition; at worst, these are features that Iberia and Latin America would rather forget and not acknowledge at all. But if these ingredients are also a part of Iberia's and Latin America's past and present, then they cannot so easily be ignored. Surely it is not up to a country or area *by itself* to decide which features of its own tradition it wishes to acknowledge and which to ignore.

The issue is complicated by strongly felt nationalistic and political sentiments. In this regard a personal story may be relevant. In 1973, while Franco was still alive, I made a scholarly presentation in Spain emphasizing the utility of using a common, culture-area approach to studying Iberia and Latin America.[9] The presentation stirred a howl of protest from Spanish writers. For at that time, at the twilight of the Franco era, Spain did not want to be considered in the same light as Latin America since that would be to emphasize authoritarianism, corporatism, and the like—all traits associated with dictatorship and the Franco regime, which most Spanish intellectuals (precisely those who attacked my presentation) wished to repudiate. Rather, Spain wanted to associate itself with "Europe," which to them meant democracy and freedom. Nor did Spain wish to be treated in the light of what it considered the backwardness, Third Worldism, and "barbarism" of Latin America. Hence, instead of confronting my argument on rational and

intellectual grounds and considering it on its merits alone, Spanish intellectuals chose to attack it purely on nationalistic, political, and, quite frankly,
racial-cultural grounds.

Some of the same sentiments were felt in Latin America but perhaps not
quite so strongly. Latin American intellectuals also wished their countries to
be considered in a light other than that of corporatism and authoritarianism
(dependency theory was then one of the more fashionable alternatives); in
addition, they sometimes resented the patronizing notion that Spain and
Portugal should be the models for them (it is the story, not unfamiliar in
North America, of former colonies eventually outdistancing their former
mother countries); nor did they see any need for Spain and Portugal to help
"orient" them into Europe when they were quite capable themselves of
dealing directly with Europe.

Even though Portugal and, especially, Spain have expanded considerably
their economic and diplomatic relations with Latin America in the past two
decades, the idea of a common cultural and sociopolitical model for both
areas is still often anathema to them. Only if the *sole* emphasis is democracy
and human rights, and only if Spain's *leadership* in these areas is acknowledged, would Spain want anything to do with such a model. For Spain now
thinks of itself as *fully* European (not two-thirds!) and wants no part of a
model that considers it in the light either of its common heritage (unless it is
selective as to which traits are emphasized) with Latin America or that
emphasizes what Spain and Portugal now think of as negative and to-be-
forgotten aspects from their past such as corporatism and authoritarianism.

The issue is complicated by the fact that many scholars who study Spain
and Portugal are also caught up in this essentially nationalistic and political
argument. For a long time to study Spain and Portugal was to study countries
with negative connotations: underdeveloped, fascistic, and on the periphery
of Europe. How much better from the point of view of these scholars to study
countries that are "democratic" and "European." In fact, as we argue here,
Spain and Portugal are still incompletely democratic and incompletely
European. But that cannot be admitted politically or intellectually since that
is to say that Iberia is still partly Latin American or partly Third World, and
still partly a product of all those traits both these countries *and* the scholars
who study them have been struggling for decades to overcome. It has been
the author's experience at various high-level conferences on Spain and
Portugal that the more uncomfortable issues raised here are thus swept under
the rug, not discussed, and ignored. More than that, the conveyors of such
uncomfortable truths that Iberia is as yet only partly democratic and that
such characteristics as patrimonialism, corporatism, and organic-statism are
still in part present must be attacked and dismissed.

But surely such views from the point of view of nationalism, politics, and mere scholarly *preference* to have one's area of interest be considered "European" rather than "Latin American" cannot be allowed to stand. At the least what is required is an honest and balanced treatment of the issues, not an out-of-hand refusal to consider them at all. If at the end of this exercise we conclude that Spain and Portugal are fully European, then so be it. But if they are still partly Latin American, then we need to acknowledge that as well. In either case, a due consideration and analysis are necessary, and not a set of conclusions arrived at *a priori*.

The Book: A Look Ahead

The chapters that follow begin to analyze, theme by theme, the arguments and issues raised in the Introduction. Chapter 2 examines the history and twentieth-century experience of Portugal with corporatism. Although the focus is on Portuguese corporatism, much of what is said in this chapter is relevant to the practice of corporatism in Spain as well and to the countries of Latin America. Of special interest is the emphasis on the distinct meanings of corporatism in different historical epochs and, because of their earlier sorry histories under Franco and Salazar, the difficulties that Spain and Portugal now have in coming to grips with modern neocorporatism.

Chapter 3 provides a broad overview of political, social, economic, and culture change in Southern Europe. Picking up where Chapter 2 leaves off, it focuses on the modernizing changes since the mid-1970s, since the end of the Franco and Salazar regimes. The chapter looks comparatively at the nations of Southern Europe (including Greece and Italy as well as Portugal and Spain) and also analyzes the likelihood of greater independence in the foreign policies of these nations.

Chapter 4 examines changing political culture in Iberia—and by extension in Latin America. It assesses how much has changed since the demise of the old regimes, and how much remains the same. Specifically, it looks at such themes as Catholicism, authoritarianism, corporatism, and patrimonialism and seeks to assess the profound earthquake in political culture since the mid-1970s. The key question, of course, is just how firmly implanted are the values and behavior that undergird democracy.

In Chapter 5 attention turns to the complex interrelations of Iberia and Latin America. The relations are not only diplomatic and economic—the normal "stuff" of foreign relations—but cultural, sociological, and highly emotional as well. The chapter assesses whether we are in a new era in

Iberia–Latin America relations and also what the implications of that are for both areas' internal politics.

Chapter 6, dealing with state-society relations, *begins* the process of trying to identify a uniquely Iberic–Latin American model of development. It focuses on the relations of the Iberic state with its component societal and corporate interests. In the case of Spain, in addition, there is a special regional component to the state-society equilibrium as well. The chapter suggests that, while Spain and Portugal have essentially become European-style parliamentary democracies, there are some special qualities to their systems of state-society relations that make them truly indigenous and distinct. Furthermore, some aspects of the Iberian model could be relevant for Latin America, which might help give democracy there a firmer basis of home-grown institutions and practices.

Chapter 7 is the transcript of a speech given on the relevance of the Iberian and Latin American transitions to democracy to Russia and Eastern Europe. Presented in 1990 at a time of optimism about democratization in Eastern Europe and Russia, the chapter emphasizes the immense difficulties involved and how Spain and Portugal had far more propitious sociopolitical bases for democracy than did Eastern Europe. Yet that is—the comparison of Southern Europe with Eastern Europe—the correct comparison, I believe, and it also offers a comparative basis for judging the chances of success of other countries embarking on similar transitions from authoritarianism to democracy.

In Chapter 8 we return to the large issues raised in the Introduction and try to provide answers to the questions raised here. These are big and important questions; not all of them can be fully answered in this space, but at least a start can be made.

Notes

1. See Howard J. Wiarda, *Latin American Politics: A New World of Possibilities* (Belmont, Calif.: Wadsworth Publishing, 1994).

2. The image is from Samuel P. Huntington, *The Third Wave: Democratization in the Late Twentieth Century* (Norman: University of Oklahoma Press, 1991). For Latin America see Howard J. Wiarda, *The Democratic Revolution in Latin America: History, Politics, and U.S. Policy* (New York: A Twentieth Century Fund Book, Holmes and Meier, 1990).

3. Francis Fukiyama, "The End of History," *The National Interest* 16 (Summer 1989).

4. Claudio Veliz, *The Centralist Tradition in Latin America* (Princeton: Princeton University Press, 1980); see also the companion volume to this book, Howard J.

Wiarda, *Democracy and Its Discontents: Development, Interdependence and U.S. Policy in Latin America* (Lanham, Md.: Rowman & Littlefield, 1995).

5. Based on data provided at Harvard University, Minda de Gunzburg Center for European Studies, Conference on "Twenty Years of Iberian Democracy: An Assessment" (Cambridge: April 7–9, 1995).

6. James Kurth et al., *Mediterranean Paradoxes: The Politics and Social Structure of Southern Europe* (Oxford, UK: Berg Publishers, 1993).

7. An excellent survey is Frederick Pike, *"Hispanismo," 1898–1936: Spanish Conservatives and Liberals and Their Relations with Spanish America* (Notre Dame: Notre Dame University Press, 1971).

8. See Howard J. Wiarda (ed.), *The Iberian-Latin American Connection: Implications for U.S. Policy* (Boulder, Colo.: Westview Press, 1986).

9. See my essay, "Interpreting Iberian–Latin American Interrelations: Paradigm Consensus and Conflict," in *The Iberian–Latin American Connection*, Chapter 8.

Chapter 2

Corporatism and Corporations: Portugal's *Estado Novo* in Historical and Comparative Perspective

Definitions

There are at least five meanings, five definitions, of the term corporatism: historical or "natural" corporatism, corporatism as ideology, corporatism as manifest politico-economic regime as in Franco's Spain or the *Estado Novo* of Dr. Antonio Salazar, modern neocorporatism, and corporatism as an explanatory paradigm in the social sciences. A dynamic relationship exists among these several forms of corporatism; however, confusion and overlap among these definitions has often rendered difficult the understanding of corporatism.

Historical or natural corporatism refers to the initial, premodern bonds that often serve as the basis for national sociopolitical organization. In India this may mean caste associations, in Africa tribe or ethnic group, in East Asia the communal bonds of Confucianism. In Iberia, the historical or natural corporations included the family, the parish, the *freguesia* (neighborhood), military orders, guilds, religious brotherhoods, towns, and universities. This definition of corporatism clearly is related to the founding of the Spanish and Portuguese states, to early state-society relations, and to deep-rooted Iberian institutions and political culture. Historical or natural corporatism of this kind was often characteristic of Southern and Western Europe from the eleventh through the fourteenth centuries.

Reprinted from Antonio Barreto and Maria Filomena Mónica (eds.), *Dicionario de Historia de Portugal* (Lisbon: Liv. Ed. Figueirinhas, 1996).

15

Corporatist ideology arose in the nineteenth century, first as a conservative reaction to the French Revolution and its abolition of the traditional corporations and later as an attempt to find a non-Marxist and nonliberal answer to the "social question": what to do about the rising power of organized labor. A manifest corporatist ideology arose initially in Germany, Austria, France, Belgium, and Italy; its popularity spread throughout Europe in the late nineteenth century and was particularly in vogue following World War I. Corporatism sought to restructure society on its presumably "natural" corporatist base and to secure (often enforce) harmony between capital and labor. There were left as well as right forms of corporatist ideology, Protestant and Catholic variations, state and societal forms. In Spain and Portugal, the most prominent currents stemmed from the papal encyclicals *Rerum Novarum* (1891) and *Quadregessimo Anno* (1931) and the Italian statist or fascist form. Corporatist ideology and corporatist regimes were most prominent in the interwar period in those countries that already had a long tradition of natural corporatism or corporatist political culture.

Corporatist regimes came to power in the period between World Wars I and II in Austria, Brazil, France, Germany, Greece, Italy, Mexico, Poland, Portugal, and Spain; other countries experimented with corporatist institutions. Considerable institutional variation existed among these corporatist regimes but most were authoritarian, sought to control the participation of organized labor and other groups in the political process, and to rationalize and regulate national economic life in the face of the world depression, the Bolshevik challenge, and the seeming unraveling in the 1930s of numerous states and societies. Most such corporative regimes were discredited by the outcome of World War II, although in Spain and Portugal a truncated corporatist system lingered until the mid-1970s.

Modern *neocorporatism* is characteristic of many industrialized, social-welfare-oriented democracies. It seeks to involve capital and labor in a tripartite arrangement with the state in such public policy areas as central planning, social security and welfare, and wage negotiations. It seeks to achieve stability and social peace through pacts that have usually involved the granting of increased wages and benefits in return for a no-strike pledge. Neocorporatism is thus compatible with the practices and institutions of democracy. Since the 1974 overthrow of the *Estado Novo* and the corporatist regime, Portugal has been moving haltingly and unevenly toward a system of neocorporatism. Spain's transition to democracy was also assisted by neocorporatist pacts involving labor unions, business, and the state.

Corporatism is not only a type of regime but it has also emerged *as a major social science paradigm*. Corporatism stands in contrast to the liberal/pluralist and Marxian paradigms but it is not necessarily incompatible with these other approaches. In this sense corporatism represents a way of thinking, a *verstehen* approach, a set of categories and institutions that help us understand distinct types of regimes, institutional arrangements, and public policy. In Portugal, corporatism was so discredited by its practice under Salazar and the denunciations of it accompanying the Revolution of Carnations that the corporatist social science approach and paradigm has been slow in developing. Spain also repudiated corporatism but continued many of its practices and institutional forms.

Early Origins

Corporatist ideology in Portugal grew in the late nineteenth and early twentieth centuries, particularly after the promulgation of *Rerum Novarum* in 1891. Procorporatist sentiment increased during the disorder of the Portuguese Republic, 1910–26; the regime of Sidónio Pais in 1917–18 was partially corporatist and served as a forerunner to the *Estado Novo*. The military government that overthrew the republic and took power in 1926 was corporatist in sentiment and mentality but lacked the ideological and political background sufficient to carry out a corporatist restructuring. Hence, its leaders turned to Antonio Salazar who had the political and economic skills and the corporatist ideology that the military lacked.

In the early 1930s Salazar as prime minister began the process of corporatist restructuring of Portuguese social, economic, and political life. Among the most important new corporatist institutions were the Constitution of 1933 with its provision for a functionally representative Corporative Chamber; the Council of State, a high-level adversary body that was also functionally representative; the Corporative Council, which was supposed to be the coordinating agency of the new corporatist regime; the Labor Statute of 1933 that regulated labor-capital relations; and the Subsecretariat (later elevated to full ministerial status) of State of Corporations and Social Welfare. The same day (September 23) that the Labor Statute was promulgated in 1933 witnessed the issuance of five major decree-laws creating a web of grass-roots corporative organizations: *gremios* for employers and patronal groups, *sindicatos* for workers, *ordens* for professional associations, *casas do povo* for farmers and peasants, and *casas dos pescadores* for fishermen. These institutions were accompanied or preceded by decrees and government actions that eliminated earlier noncorporatist agencies such as the trade unions, sometimes accompanied by violence and repression. The nominal capstones of the corporative systems, the corporations themselves, which were supposed to integrate capital and labor and to be key agencies in establishing social and economic policy, did not come into existence until 1957, twenty-four years after the creation of the other corporative institutions.

The influences on Portuguese corporatism derived from several sources. *Quadregesimo Anno* was particularly important in 1931 in stimulating the group of Catholic intellectuals (Salazar, Marcello Caetano, Teotonio Pereira) who drafted the early legislation. The Labor Statute was almost a direct translation of Mussolini's *Carta del Lavoro*. In France, Spain, Germany, Italy, and Belgium there was already a vast corporatist literature on which to draw. But Portuguese corporatism was mainly conservative, statist, and Catholic; it never drew from, and was bitterly opposed to, the left-wing corporatism of Trotsky, the Italian Marxist corporatists, or the regime of Lázaro Cárdenas in Mexico. At the same time the Salazar regime rejected the violent and extreme right-wing views of Antonio Sardinha and his fascist *Integralismo Lusitano* and took strong steps to suppress it.

While the political institutions of corporatism have received major attention, of at least equal importance were the economic institutions, which are far less well known. These were the Organizations of Economic Coordination of which there were three types: Regulatory Commissions, which regulated imports, National Juntas, which regulated exports, and Institutes, which guaranteed the quality of Portuguese products. The varied Organizations of Economic Coordination assisted the Salazar regime in rationalizing and regulating the economy; they also served, in the midst of the world depression, as the means by which the state extended its influence over virtually every sector of the economy. These organizations helped set wages, prices, and production; they also served as a method by which a more centralized and authoritarian *state corporatism* supplanted the earlier (at least in theory) corporatism of free associability.

Implementation

Once put formally in place in the early 1930s, many of the corporative institutions herein described (the Organizations of Economic Coordination excepted) lingered on the vine for many years and were seldom implemented or grew into important decision-making bodies. The postponement of implementation was due to the several crises the regime faced: the world depression of the 1930s, opposition from labor and business groups that did not want to be restructured along corporatist lines, the Spanish Civil War, World War II and the discrediting (because of their association with fascism and Nazism) of all such corporatist regimes, the continued economic poverty of Portugal, which made further corporatist implementation seem risky, and finally, after

World War II, uncertainty on the part of the Salazar regime as to whether it would go further with the corporatist restructuring. The "corporatist revolution of 1933" largely came to a standstill.

Hence, during the 1940s and on into the 1950s the regime—and its corporatist institutions—stagnated. This was a period of severe economic backwardness in Portugal, of isolation from the counsels of Europe because of its supposedly "fascist" institutions, and of uncertainty on the part of Salazar as to the future directions of the country. The regime stagnated until the economic recovery of the mid-1950s began to lift the country out of depression.

The Corporatist Revival

After two decades of stagnation, the corporative system underwent a revival in the mid-1950s. Leading the campaign were the *Gabinete de Estudos Corporativos*, its *Revista*, a handful of Catholic intellectuals and scholars, and ultimately Salazar himself. These intellectuals advanced the argument for the completion of the corporative system and for a return to the early principles of corporatism of free associability rather than corporatism of the state, which was an indirect criticism of governmental authoritarianism. As a result of this campaign, a bill authorizing the creation of the corporations, the final stage in the corporatist edifice, was submitted in 1956 and enacted in 1957. The first six corporations were organized around major economic activities: agriculture, industry, commerce, credit and insurance, fishing and canning, and transport and tourism. Two new corporations, for press and printing and for entertainment, were added in 1959, and three more in 1966: welfare; science, letters and arts; and physical education and sports. Since there was by now little enthusiasm for the extension of corporations to other areas, such as religion or the military, this wave of legislation was widely recognized as representing the final step in the corporatist experiment.

Each corporation was supposed to consist of an equal number of representatives from both workers' and employers' organizations but in fact state interests and those of employers usually dominated. The corporations were supposed to serve as intermediaries between the grass-roots organizations and the state, but in practice they seldom served that function either. They were given broad powers in law to regulate the economy for the common good, although for the most part the state continued to be the chief regulator and the corporations saw their role limited to enforcement of labor and economic regulations and to technical areas that mainly benefitted the business community: market surveys, studies, and economic reports. The functions of the corporations remained extremely circumscribed.

Meanwhile, under a succession of able administrators and with Salazar's blessings, the Corporations subsecretariat was revived. First, the subsecretariat was elevated to full ministerial status; second, it was renamed as the Ministry of Corporations and Social Welfare; and third, it was given a variety of new responsibilities. As the Portuguese economy began to expand in the late 1950s, early 1960s; as popular demands for more and better social services increased; and as it became clear that traditional religious and family charity was no longer adequate to serve the needs of a more urban and impersonal society, the Salazar regime determined to radically shift the purpose and functions of the moribund corporatist system. It never repudiated the original corporatist goals, purposes, and ideology; but it did reorient the entire corporatist system toward becoming a European-style social welfare agency. Henceforth there would be little mention of corporatism as a system of class harmony or as an alternative to liberalism and socialism; instead the new focus was almost entirely on social welfare.

Many of the new social programs having to do with social security, health care, adult education, retirement programs, unemployment insurance, welfare, etc., continued to exist mainly on paper; and the rising opposition, including the underground socialist and communist organizations, were quick to point out the many deficiencies. But Portugal was still a poor country by European standards and it could not afford all these new programs; nevertheless a start was made, which fueled the demand for still more programs. Hence, during the 1960s the corporative system, especially the Corporations Ministry, was converted into a large social welfare apparatus, not all that different from social welfare ministries in other countries. Some feeble efforts were made to convert the lower-level corporative agencies—the casas do povo, casas dos pescadores, sindicatos, etc.—into agencies to carry out these new social programs; but few of them served that role and hence the web of grass-roots corporative bodies created in the early 1930s fell into even greater disuse. Many were abandoned altogether. Only the gremios functioned more or less well, rather like business associations and often in collaboration with the corporations and the appropriate government regulatory agencies; but even they were often resented by their own members as inefficient, bureaucratic, and getting in the way of private profit-making.

Corporatism under Caetano

Marcello Caetano, Salazar's successor beginning in 1968, thought of himself as a reformer and a "liberal," but liberal only within the corporatist tradition. He loosened the reins of authoritarianism and state control some-what and allowed greater degrees of freedom in Portugal; but he never abandoned corporatism and, while his authoritarianism was not so hard or rigid as Salazar's, the Portuguese regime remained an authoritarian one. Caetano's goal was to modernize corporatism and to continue and enhance the program of social welfare carried out through the Ministry of Corpora-tions. He never repudiated corporatism or, for that matter, the web of controls inherited from Salazar's dictatorship; but he did preside over a softer, more humane, somewhat liberalized version of the corporative state.

Meanwhile, under Caetano as under Salazar, the real locus of power in the regime was located elsewhere, not in the corporative complex of institu-tions. These other power centers included the secret police, the armed forces, the prime minister's office, the presidency, the high bureaucracy, and the industrial-banking sector—often organized as *grupos*, which were really holding companies, and included most of the wealthy elite families of Portugal, who frequently had holdings in Portuguese Africa as well as Continental Portugal. Indeed, in an interview with the prime minister conducted by the author, the prime minister indicated that he had to move slowly both on Africa policy and in reforming domestic policy because he would otherwise be overthrown immediately by powerful vested interests.

The Revolution

The revolution of 1974–75 began as a quite conservative and limited revolution aimed at deposing Caetano and changing Portugal's Africa policy, but it soon became more radical and with a much broader agenda. Not only was Caetano sent into exile but in a series of decrees issued by a succession of revolutionary governments in 1974–75 the entire edifice of the corporative system came tumbling down. The Corporative Chamber, the Corporative Council, the Council of State, the Corporations, *Sindicatos*, *Ordens*, and *Gremios* were all abolished in rapid succession by decree law. The Corpora-tions Ministry became the Ministry of Labor, although many of its functions remained the same. All these corporative institutions were associated with "fascism" in the 1970s and therefore they had to be repudiated and destroyed.

There were, of course, many problems associated with the corporative institutions of the 1960s and 1970s. But in many cases these institutions were eliminated in the course of the revolution before any new or better ones were created, leaving Portugal even worse off than before. In addition, because corporatism was so strongly associated with fascism, the corporative institu-tions were abolished largely on ideological grounds, thus ignoring the reforms in the system and its reorientation toward useful social welfare programs in the 1960s and 1970s. The corporative system was abolished in the heat and ideological passion of a revolutionary context, not as the result of a careful assessment of both its limits and its accomplishments.

In 1974–75 Portugal repudiated the corporatist ideology of the Salazar regime, its corporatist political and economic institutions, and much of the country's historic, corporatist-organicist political culture. But in much of Europe and other advanced countries during precisely this same period, corporatism in its societal or neocorporatist forms was being rediscovered and often celebrated. Neocorporatism involves the coming together under state auspices of both labor and capital to work out policy for social welfare, wages, planning, technological change, and other public policy issues. Modern neocorporatism is quite compatible with democracy, pluralism, and social justice. But because Portugal had just been engaged in a revolution aimed, among other things, at repudiating corporatism in all its manifestations, it was not prepared to embrace neocorporatism. The result often was dysfunction: rejecting corporatism at one level while continuing to practice it, often surreptitiously or in disguised form, at others; remaining suspicious of all collaborative arrangements between capital and labor; embracing Marxian concepts of class conflict whereas in the rest of Europe there was great emphasis on social pacts; *et cetera*. The repudiation of corporatism in Portugal was so strong stemming from the revolution and the discredited Salazar regime that for a long time (and still today, in some quarters) any kind of corporatism was considered anathema.

Parallel developments occurred within the social sciences. Even though, globally, corporatist analyses, paradigms, and intellectual approaches have now taken their place alongside Marxism and liberal/pluralism as among the leading social science approaches, in Portugal, because of this earlier history, corporatist approaches to studying labor relations, social welfare policy, and a variety of other issues are still largely politically incorrect. Corporatism in *all* forms and for *whatever* purposes must be repudiated because of its association with the former regime. One understands why this is so, and the phenomenon of knee-jerk anticorporatism will certainly fade with time; but meanwhile, because of this all-encompassing rejection of corporatism, Portugal is missing out on some important new developments in the social, economic, political, and scholarly fields.

Corporatist developments in Spain often ran parallel to those in Portugal. There was a long history of "natural" or premodern corporatism, then the impact of the French Revolution and Napoleon and the emergence of corporatist ideological movements, a short and unhappy experience with republicanism followed by civil war and the manifestly corporatist regime of

Generalissimo Francisco Franco. But Franco was more a pragmatist and less a corporatist "true believer" than Salazar, and hence in Spain corporatism was less thoroughly implemented or given much influence than it was in Portugal. After Franco's death in 1975 the corporatist institutions he had put in place were repudiated (they had long been in decline) as Spain began its transition to democracy. But Spain continued many corporatist practices while at the same time moving partially toward neocorporatism and employing some limited modes of corporatist social science interpretation.

Suggested Readings

Caetano, Marcello. *O sistema corporativa* (Lisbon: O Jornal do Comercio e das Colonias, 1938).

Cardoso, J. Pires. *O Corporativismo como ideologia para o occidente* (Lisbon, 1961).

Lucena, Manuel de. *A Evolução do sistema corporativa Portugues*, 2 vols., *O Salazarism, O Marcelismo* (Lisbon: Perspectives e realidades, 1976).

Manoilesco, Mihail. *Le Siecle du corporatisme* (Paris: Felix Alcan, 1934).

Revista do Grabinete de Estudos Corporativos, various issues.

Salazar, Antonio de Oliveira. *Revolução Corporativa* (Oporto: Diario do Norte, 1960).

Wiarda, Howard J. *Corporatism and Development: The Portuguese Experience* (Amherst: University of Massachusetts Press, 1977).

———. *Politics in Iberia: The Political Systems of Spain and Portugal* (New York: HarperCollins, 1992).

———, with Iêda Siqueira Wiarda. *The Transition to Democracy in Spain and Portugal* (Lanham, Md.: University Press of America, 1987).

Chapter 3

Politics and Social Change in Southern Europe: Toward Greater Independence?

With all the attention focused recently on the changes in the Soviet Union, Eastern Europe, and Central Europe (mainly, German unification), we have not devoted sufficient scrutiny to Southern Europe.[1] But, in fact, the changes there—although occurring out of the headlines—may be just as significant in long-range terms.

Southern Europe is undergoing immense cultural, economic, social, and political transformation. These domestic changes also carry immense international implications, which may well lead to greater independence and some new directions in the foreign policies of the Southern European nations. The changes, therefore, carry major implications for U.S. foreign policy.

Culture Changes

Southern European culture is alive and vibrant. The attention to culture has been enormously stimulated by the new prosperity of Southern Europe in recent decades and by the success of the Southern European countries' political transitions to democracy and stability. Italy led the way in the post–World War II period and has long had an intensely creative culture; now, since the movement against the colonels in Greece, the Portuguese Revolution in 1974, and the death of Franco in Spain in 1975, cultural innovation in these three countries has also been impressive. Music, the arts,

Published in *Current History* (November 1991).

theater, book publishing, film, architecture, education, and research are all flourishing.

Perhaps the most creative renaissance has been occurring in Barcelona, which may be the most dynamic city in Europe. Barcelona was spruced up for the 1992 Olympics as well as the celebration of the 500th anniversary of Columbus's discovery of America. About two billion dollars was spent on stadiums, hotels, museums, and restaurants; a Joan Miró sculpture towers over the city. The world's best-known architects are producing an orgy of creativity; theater, dance, and music extravaganzas are turning the city into a haven of culture. Barcelona's explosion of culture only slightly surpasses similar flowerings in Rome, Milan, Athens, Madrid, Lisbon, and a surprisingly large number of regional cities.

Immense changes in the political culture are also underway. Greece's once prosperous monasteries are manned now by handfuls of tired old men; in Italy, Spain, and Portugal the process of secularization is similarly well underway. In these three countries the Catholic Church has been gravely weakened as a cultural and political institution. In Portugal, still the most traditional of the countries, the percentage of active, practicing Catholics is down to about 15 percent of the population; in Italy and Spain the percentages are about half that.

Not only is it no longer possible for the Church to dictate public policy, but the Church is so weak politically that it could not even block legislation in Spain and Portugal permitting divorce and family planning. Italy, Spain, and Portugal are no longer "Catholic political cultures" as they once were, grounded on notions of Thomistic authority and hierarchy. Rather they have become primarily secular, universalistic in their values, urban, and materialistic—just like the rest of Europe. They want jeans, Coca-Cola, freedom, and rock music. They have been thoroughly caught up in the global political culture of democracy and consumerism, and it is inconceivable at this stage that the clock could be turned back. In the historic conflict between the "two Spains," "two Portugals," "two Greeces," and "two Italies," the modern, secular, democratic one has now definitively triumphed.

As traditional and premodern Spain, Portugal, Italy, and Greece have faded or disappeared, interest is, however, growing at the level of history and nostalgia in the "old country" that is disappearing. This is a remarkable change since, in the past, the conflicts between the old and the new in these countries wrent the nation's soul and often produced conflict, instability, and, in Spain, civil war. But now it appears in Greece, Spain, and Portugal, and in Italy several decades ago, that the modern, urban, democratic, secular, and European-oriented sector has clearly won out over the religious, rural, conservative, traditionalist, and inward-looking sector. The transition is now sufficiently complete that much of premodern Spain or Greece or Portugal seems on the verge of disappearing.

The Spain, Portugal, and Greece of the Middle Ages now exists chiefly in isolated rural areas and small villages. It is premodern, highly traditionalist, and intensely religious. It represents a residual part of these countries that is still dominated by religious determinism and spectacles, by a sense of the absolute, by rigidly drawn social lines, and by a sense of fatalism and of the preordained. But this Spain, this Greece, this Italy, and this Portugal are fast disappearing, giving way to more cosmopolitan attitudes and institutions. These culture changes have also been reflected in the political sphere where a "subject" political culture is giving way to a more democratic and participatory one.[2]

Economic Change

These culture changes have been powerfully fueled by the economic transformation of Southern Europe in recent decades. Southern Europe is becoming prosperous and even affluent for the first time. A culture of poverty is giving way to a culture of consumerism and material goods. Poverty still exists in Southern Europe as it does in other modern countries but now we talk chiefly of pockets of poverty rather than an entire, society-wide culture of poverty.

Italy once again leads the way. Italy has become so prosperous that it surprises (*il sorpasso*) even the Italians. Italy has one of the liveliest and most dynamic economies in the world. During the 1980s, when many other economies were in on-again, off-again recession, Italy boomed ahead at growth rates averaging 3.9 percent per year—among Europe's highest. When economists two years ago reassessed Italian finances to take into account the vast underground economy, Italy had surpassed Great Britain as the fifth largest economy in the world and was approaching the gross national product of France, which ranked fourth. Even the South of Italy, the *Mezzogiorno*, historically its poorest region, is now benefitting from the boom. Italy is brimming with economic self-confidence and a sense of well-being, and most economists expect respectable growth to continue for the next several years.

Spain has been the other economic "miracle" in Southern Europe. During the 1960s after Franco freed up the economy by reducing its autarkic features, Spanish economic growth was second only to Japan in the world. Spain's per capita income doubled—and then doubled again. Like Italy, even in the recessionary 1980s Spain continued to boom. Spain's spurt was sustained even under a Socialist government, which proved to be nonthreatening to business. When Spain formally joined the European Economic Community (EEC) in 1986, the economy received another stimulus since Spain qualified for considerable European assistance and received massive new investment. With all the new factories, employing women as well as men, middle-class Spaniards began complaining of a shortage of maids. Spain experienced a brief downturn and high unemployment in the early 1990s as the world economy also faltered, but no one expected the Spanish economy to remain in the doldrums for long. There is too much dynamism, construction, and *movimiento* in Spain for that.

Portugal's economy has not performed as well as Italy's or Spain's, but it has been impressive nonetheless. After the revolution and upheaval of the 1970s, Portugal's government settled down and became more stable and moderate in the 1980s, becoming more attractive to investment. Portugal's joining the EEC in 1986 provided an enormous impetus to the economy, perhaps even more so than for Spain. Portugal received considerable subsidies and new investment began to pour into the country. Hence, the economy boomed even during the recession years of the late 1980s. But the subsidies will end soon, and there is considerable fear in Portugal that its small-sized and family-based firms will not be able to compete with the European giants. Portugal is in for a period of adjustment, even though economic growth is expected to continue.

Greece has been the odd country out in this picture of general Southern European prosperity. After a decade of chaotic socialist rule under Prime Minister Andreas Papandreou, the Greek economy was the weakest of any in the EEC and was approaching Third World status. The country has a vast welfare system that hardly functions, an inflated and inefficient public sector, and is rife with patronage and corruption.

When Papandreou and the Socialists were defeated in 1990 by a conservative coalition headed by Constantine Mitsotakis, observers expected the economic conditions to improve. But Mitsotakis proved to be very cautious in tackling the country's economic problems. He had only a one-seat majority in the parliament, and the left and the unions in Greece are formidable foes. Greece has a very high budget deficit, high unemployment (9 percent), and an inflation rate over 20 percent. The economy continued to deteriorate, and Greece spiraled down to pass Portugal as the poorest country in the EEC. Economists thought that with the election of a more conservative government Greece would attract foreign investment, but the chaotic conditions continued and the anticipated investment failed to materialize. The EEC pressured Greece as a condition of new loans to cut its budget deficit, cut inflation, and reduce its bloated public sector; some but probably very limited progress was expected from the cautious Mitsotakis. Conditions deteriorated so badly that in 1993 Papandreou was able to make a comeback.

Social Change

The economic boom in Southern Europe over the past forty years has given rise to vast social changes and to a new kind of society whose precise character is still uncertain.

The countryside is emptying of people as more and more Greeks, Spaniards, Portuguese, and Italians flock to the cities and regions of jobs and greater prosperity. The historic "peasant problem" (poverty, lack of progress) of these societies is being "solved" by this exodus from the rural areas, since there are very few peasants left. Old people, women, and children are being left behind in the rural villages—and now the women are beginning to migrate too. Peasant agriculture is disappearing; larger, sometimes corporate farms are taking over. Albeit more slowly, rural areas are beginning to share in the greater prosperity and new social programs emanating from the capital cities; there has been some "trickle down." But a peasant and rural "way of life"—slower, more conservative—is disappearing, never to be revived. Even the smaller regional centers now have vast new shopping centers, factories, and employment. More slowly in Greece and Portugal, more rapidly in Italy and Spain, an entire rural way of life is fading. Meanwhile the newly affluent city dwellers are "rediscovering their roots" by buying land and homes for weekend retreats back in the areas from which they came.

A second major change involves gender roles. Women are now working for salaries as never before. Poorer women get jobs as secretaries, store clerks, or in the factories; they dress better and are healthier than before, and they have money to spend. Middle- and upper-class women are joining the professions, and in all the countries women are at or approaching 50 percent of the university student bodies. Frequently these working women are bringing home checks that are larger than their husbands', giving rise to large problems of ego, *machismo*, and the management of the family's funds. New questions are being raised about day care and who will look out for the children (still largely aunts and grandmothers). At the same time traditional family relationships are being upset and divorce is becoming more prevalent. The historic patriarchal family is undergoing transformation.

A third change involves the generations. Nowhere are the generation gaps larger than in Southern Europe, especially Portugal and Spain. Because of the long (forty years) Salazar and Franco dictatorships in these two countries, there are actually two generational differences, both of which had to be bridged at once. The first was toward a new generation of politicians and bureaucrats, people in their thirties, forties, and fifties, who had long been eager to inherit power from the aging dinosaurs, as Franco and Salazar were called. That shift in power was largely accomplished in the 1970s through the transition to democracy in both countries. But at the same time there was a second generation of young people, oriented toward pleasure and consumerism and often uninterested in the great political issues of the day. They are like young people everywhere in their devotion to rock music, freedom from all constraints, and new modes of dress and conduct. They are often a mystery not only to the old Franco/Salazar generation but also to the second generation that has inherited responsibility since then.

Meanwhile, in all the countries of the region but especially Italy, a new, ambitious entrepreneurial spirit has emerged—and a new entrepreneurial class. Italy has literally hundreds of thousands of new small, flexible, imaginative businesses characterized by a willingness to work hard and take risks. Their profits are often augmented by the fact that they operate at the margins of the underground economy. These highly competitive new companies are quite different from the state-protected monopolies and oligopolies of the past.

The students have been largely quiescent since the "hot summer" in 1969 in Italy and the Portuguese Revolution of 1974. Like their national societies, the students are more serious, calmer, and less politicized. Greece's students tend to be more activist because of that country's divisive economic and political situation, and Italy has experienced a resurgence of campus protests triggered by inadequate facilities in the crowded campuses and by a government plan to have the universities sign contracts with large industrial firms. But it is doubtful that the protests will have society-wide reverberations as they had in the 1960s.

The unions have been energetic in all four Southern European countries, but only Greece has had a prolonged wave of strikes. In Italy the workers are doing better than ever before and many are joining the middle class; in Spain a series of social pacts providing for higher wages in return for a no-strike pledge has been signed among the state, employers, and the unions; and in Portugal new jobs and rising affluence have undercut the former militancy of the unions. As wages and working conditions have improved, communist strength in the unions has declined and the socialist (and Christian-Democratic, in Italy) unions have emerged as the most numerous. The intense class conflict of a generation ago has ameliorated.

All of Southern Europe has now become more middle class. The middle class dominates in such institutions as the parties, the bureaucracy, the unions, the Church, business, and the military. Although there are still major class differences, the social gaps between rich and poor are not so apparent as before. Meantime, the new middle class in all these countries seems to provide a more solid basis for democracy and stability than ever before.

Democratization

In the past two decades the countries of Southern Europe (Greece, Portugal, Spain, Turkey too) have gone through a remarkable process of democratization. Italy democratized earlier, after World War II, following the fall of Mussolini; now, after a series of political scandals, it is redemocratizing, deepening its democracy. Democratization of Southern Europe is one of the great accomplishments of the late twentieth century and is comparable in importance to the unification of Germany and the changes occurring in Eastern Europe and the former Soviet Union. Southern Europe's democratization of the mid-1970s also provided a model for the democratic openings in Latin America, East Asia, and, now, worldwide.

The Portuguese Revolution of 1974 overthrew the Salazar/Caetano regime and ushered in a period of turmoil and instability. But eventually the country settled down and became less frenetic. In 1987 under Aníbal Cavaco Silva the Social Democratic Party (PSD) won an absolute majority in the Portuguese parliament, the first time any party had done that since the Revolution. The PSD competes with the Socialist Party (PS) and the Communist Party (now in decline) on the left and with the Social Democratic Center (CDS, the Christian-Democratic Party) on the right. With the economy prospering, centrist government (PSD or PS) or a centrist coalition seems likely to continue in Portugal.

Spain following Franco's death in 1975 went through a *reforma*, as distinct from the *ruptura* experienced by Portugal. Franco's ministers were replaced by the centrist Adolfo Suárez; his party in turn yielded in 1982 to the Socialist Party (PSOE) of Felipe González. González, young and charismatic, served as prime minister for over a decade. Meanwhile the Spanish Right, once powerful, went into decline, and the center has been divided. Various efforts have been underway to revive a center-right coalition, now organized as the People's Party (PP) and gaining in popularity. González's government, though generally "clean," has been charged recently with corruption; and after being in power for over ten years the PSOE government has antagonized various groups.

In August 1974, the Greek colonels left power, yielding to democratic government. The Greek monarchy (the monarchy in Spain had played a crucial transitional role in the evolution toward democracy) was also abolished. Since then, Greece has oscillated between right and left. Conservative elements dominated in the first few years and Greece remained largely stable; then beginning in 1981 Andreas Papandreou and his Socialist Party (PASOK) governed over the course of a tumultuous decade; and in April 1990 the conservative New Democracy Party under Mitsotakis returned to power. But Greece remains polarized politically (Papandreou came back again in 1993), the middle class is divided, class conflict is rampant, and Greece remains dependent on outside aid: financial assistance from the EEC and support from the United States. So far, these conflicts have not moderated nor has the political system settled down as it has elsewhere in Southern Europe.

Italy's political system, referred to as the *"circus maximus,"* is, of course, *sui generis.* It is both a source of wonderment to outside observers and often to the Italians (who refer to it as *"lo spettacolo,"* the "spectacle") *and* a possible model for the rest of Southern Europe. Although Italy has had fifty governments since World War II and thus seems unstable, it has had only nineteen prime ministers (some have served several times). In addition, the bureaucracy, the political class, and the state system have remained stable even while cabinets have frequently come and gone. Moreover, the Italian government has been successful in the big things: it has helped provide unprecedented prosperity, it had repulsed the strong communist challenge, it has beaten back terrorism, and it provides vast patronage coupled with social services. So perhaps the Italian political system, in its own messy and chaotic way, has not been so inefficient after all. Nevertheless, the sense is growing that the system has become bloated, corrupt, and unresponsive, too much dominated by patronage and the art of making deals behind closed doors, and in need of institutional reform. No one is quite certain what form such institutional reforms will take: a stronger presidency or perhaps a less intense party faction (or even new parties) and interest group struggle are being talked of. But others argue that since the country is doing so well economically, why tamper too much with the system now.

In 1985 *all* the countries of Southern Europe, including France, had socialist governments. Some were more militant than others, and the Portuguese government was a coalition arrangement; still, with socialists in power in all the countries and Italy then seeming to be moving toward the long-anticipated "historic compromise" with the Communist Party (PCI), it appeared that socialism in Southern Europe would be the wave of the future. But since the mid-1980s Portugal and Greece have elected more centrist governments, Italy backed away from the historic compromise and the PCI went into decline, and it seems just a matter of time before a center-right coalition or movement in Spain replaces González and the PSOE.

These political changes have helped ensure economic prosperity in Southern Europe, have resulted in a repudiation of the extreme left, have helped ensure more stable politics, and have probably strengthened democracy. At this point Southern Europe seems stabler and with a brighter future than ever before.

Foreign Policy and Strategic Implications

The very prosperity, stability, and, now, democratic legitimacy that Southern Europe enjoys has enabled the area and its individual countries to play a more independent foreign policy role than previously. With the Cold War now over and the Soviet/Communist threat gone, Southern Europe no longer feels menaced and the Cold War preoccupations and pressures have disappeared. Hence, Southern Europe feels it can strike out on its own as never before.

First, Southern Europe now considers itself (almost) fully European. This is especially true of prosperous Italy but it has also become true of Greece, Spain, and Portugal. Southern Europe is part of Europe not just economically and politically but socially, culturally, and psychologically as well. No longer, as the old saws had it, does Europe stop at the Pyrenees or the Alps. Greece no longer lies "beyond the pale" (Talleyrand). Full integration into Europe likely means further distancing from the United States politically and psychologically.

Second and related, Southern Europe is questioning NATO and the Atlantic Alliance as never before. Southern Europe has always considered itself distant from any potential Central European conflict, and now with the dissolution of the Warsaw Pact it feels even less anxiety. Greece signed, in July 1990, a new eight-year pact allowing continued use of the U.S. military bases in the country in return for one billion dollars in military assistance; and Spain, Portugal, and Italy will similarly be renewing their bases agreements. Nevertheless, there is a great deal of public and official ambivalence about the bases in all four countries, and a strong sense that they are no longer so needed. Hence, we are likely to see more reductions in the size of the American units stationed at these bases, reductions in fighter squadrons (as occurred in Spain), greater restrictions on the storage of nuclear or chemical weapons, etc. Meanwhile, Southern Europe will also be deeply involved in the rethinking about NATO that is going on all over Europe, and in its restructuring or the finding of alternatives.

A third trend is toward closer relations among the Southern European countries themselves. Not only is Southern Europe now more closely integrated into the European Community (EC) but within the EC the nations of this area have begun to see themselves as a special subregional caucus—rather like the Scandinavian nations do. There are now regular meetings of the Southern European prime ministers, regular exchanges between ministries and specialized government agencies, vastly expanded cultural exchanges, greater tourism, more joint business ventures, etc. Southern Europe has not exactly become a "bloc" in any formal sense but there is widespread recognition of a certain common "Mediterranean" cultural heritage and of linked if not common issues and problems.

Finally, there are new, often linked, out-of-area issues. The Mediterranean Sea, with its problems of pollution, overlapping fishing rights, etc., provides one set of common issues. In addition, in part relating to immigration, in part to oil needs, and in part to a greater flow of commerce, drugs, and tourism, all the Southern European countries have in the past few years forged closer and generally more cooperative relations with the nations of North Africa than they had maintained before. Since all the Southern European countries are large oil importers, moreover, they are very worried about the situation in the Middle East, want the conflicts there to be resolved, strongly support the finding of a homeland for the Palestinians, and tend to tilt toward the Arab states more than toward Israel. In the same vein, they *all* would like to see the long-festering Greco-Turkish conflict ameliorated and these two countries' dispute over Cyprus settled. Political disintegration in the Balkans, especially Yugoslavia, is also worrisome from Southern Europe's point of view since it may be disruptive of their own still-shaky political and economic situations and could stimulate ethnic separation (especially in Spain) within their own borders. Meanwhile, Spain is pursuing a more forceful Latin America policy, Portugal is rediscovering Africa, and Italy's rising economic importance is reflected in a stronger role in various international forums.

All of these trends in Southern Europe point toward greater independence from U.S. policy, greater regionalism, and more assertiveness on the part of the Southern European nations in pursuing their own foreign policy priorities. In our concentration on the changes in Eastern and Central Europe, we have largely neglected what is occurring in Southern Europe; but it is plain we will need to address these issues and that understanding of Southern Europe's perspectives and creative diplomacy on the United States's part will be required.

Conclusion

Southern Europe, with Italy leading the way but with Spain, Portugal, and Greece now following, has made enormous strides in recent decades.

Vast cultural, social, economic, and political changes are under way that have fundamentally altered the appearance and institutions of Southern Europe. In summary terms, these changes may be described as providing for far greater social differentiation and pluralism, widespread economic development and industrialization, vast social modernization, and political development and democratization. Southern Europe, while still retaining many of its distinctive ways, has become fully *European*, with all that term implies.

The transition to modernity and democracy in Southern Europe is one of the late-twentieth century's most significant and heartening developments. At the same time, we must recognize that such vast modernization, coming at the same time as the end of the Cold War and vast changes internationally, leads to new foreign policy issues and concerns as well. As Southern Europe has become more affluent and as the political systems of the area have stabilized, their governments have begun to pursue more activist and independent foreign policies. These new foreign policies and the new priorities and issues involved will also require understanding and a creative response from the rest of Europe and the United States.[3]

Notes

1. The definition of Southern Europe used here is that of the EEC: Greece, Italy, Portugal, and Spain; however, France, Turkey, and Yugoslavia are also briefly mentioned.

2. The terms stem from Gabriel Almond and Sidney Verba, *The Civic Culture* (Princeton: Princeton University Press, 1963); see also Edward Banfield, *The Moral Basis of a Backward Society* (Glencoe, Ill.: The Free Press, 1958).

3. For an earlier treatment of many of these themes, see the Special Issue on "Southern Europe and the Mediterranean" of the *AEI Foreign Policy and Defense Review*, Vol. 6, No. 2 (1986) containing topical as well as country-by-country analyses by Eric N. Baklanoff, Thomas Bruneau, Edward A. Kolodziej, Keith Legg, Stanley Payne, Robert Putnam, and the present author.

Chapter 4

Changing Political Culture in Iberia—And by Extension in Latin America

Spain and Portugal have by now made some remarkable *political* transitions to democracy. In the years since the death of Franco and the deposition of the Salazar/Caetano regime, political parties have competed for elective office, elections have been held regularly, the parliament has developed, and all the institutional machinery of democracy has been put in place. There is no doubt that Spain and Portugal are now governed more democratically than at any time in the preceding forty years—or maybe ever.

The question we must now ask is, How much has the underlying political culture of Iberia changed? Granted that the institutions of democracy have been put in place, but does that mean that historic Spanish and Portuguese attitudes and behavior have been altered? Spain and Portugal have long been known as countries where authoritarianism, elitism, and paternalism are deeply embedded, not only in the political tradition from Isabella and Ferdinand through Franco and Salazar but in social and cultural attitudes and institutions as well. Personal values, the Church, the family, the social order, and other institutions have long been based on mores and beliefs that are as authoritarian as those in the political realm. Indeed, these authoritarian belief systems have long undergirded the authoritarian political order. So, while Spain and Portugal have put the formal institutions of democracy in place, unless underlying attitudes change correspondingly, Iberian democracy could quickly be in deep trouble. That is the question we explore here: Just how much have Spanish and Portuguese attitudes, belief systems, values,

Published in Howard J. Wiarda, *Politics in Iberia: The Political Systems of Spain and Portugal* (New York: HarperCollins, 1992).

and political behavior been altered to go along with the obvious changes in the political-institutional realm? The answer is crucially important to our assessment of the prospects for Iberian—and Latin American—democracy.

Political Culture as an Explanatory Device

Anthropologist Clifford Geertz has defined culture as "the structures of meaning through which men give shape to their experience."[1] Edgar Schein also provides a good summary definition of culture as "a pattern of basic assumptions—invented, discovered, or developed by a group as it learns to cope with its problems of external adaptation and internal integration—that has worked well enough to be considered valid and, therefore, to be taught to new members as the correct way to perceive, think, and feel in relation to these problems."[2] Especially noteworthy in this second definition is not just the concept of shared assumptions within a culture but how these may be passed on from generation to generation, often for hundreds of years.

Here we are concerned mainly with *political* culture—that is, with those attitudes and orientations within the general culture that specifically affect political institutions and behavior. We will be examining the shared assumptions of the Iberian nations, the beliefs and values that shape the political system, the artifacts and symbols (flags, anthems, agencies) of national identity, and the patterns of political behavior of the Spanish and Portuguese. We will also discuss subcultures that may exist within the overall political culture, as well as the processes of cultural continuity and change.

Political culture has sometimes been a troubling concept in the field of comparative political studies.[3] We can talk of, examine, and measure *patterns* of political culture, but we need to guard against that tailing off into dangerous national stereotyping or even racism. At the same time, advocates of economic determinist approaches often dismiss political culture as merely a part of the "superstructure," a reflection of underlying economic or class interests without explanatory power of its own. Another problem is that political culture can become a residual category, a "dumping ground" of explanations ("Oh, it's because they're Spanish!") when we have no other means of explanation.

Most serious scholars, however, argue that we cannot understand Iberia without taking into account Catholicism and the historic role of the Catholic Church, the educational and family systems and how values are taught, the historical tradition of Spain and Portugal, social attitudes among the classes (i.e., the traditional upper-class disdain for manual labor), the role of law and the code law legal system, political institutions and attitudes toward authority, and other features long dominant in Spain and Portugal. But, of course, as soon as we talk of *any* of these things, we are necessarily talking of political culture. Political culture is undoubtedly important; the only real question is *how* important.

Is it the political culture that shapes or determines the economic processes and political institutions of Iberia, or is it economic and institutional forces that shape and determine the political culture? Put in social science terms, is political culture a *dependent variable* (dependent on economic or institutional forces) or an *independent* one, standing on its own? Which came first, the chicken or the egg?

The answer is both—and at the same time it may be a silly and unnecessary question. It is very obvious in Spanish and Portuguese history that at some points the political culture variables (let us say Catholicism and the Catholic Church) shaped political and economic outcomes, whereas at other times (the past three decades) socioeconomic forces have been determinant in altering the culture.[4]

Political culture is, therefore, both an independent and a dependent variable at the same time: Political culture both helps determine economic and political outcomes and at the same time is itself changed by them. Nor is it necessary to answer the chicken-egg problem; rather, we should see political culture, geographic factors, economic forces, political forces, and international pressures all interacting in interrelated, complex, and dynamic ways. Political culture is, thus, a useful and necessary but not a complete or sufficient explanatory factor; we must also recognize that it is not fixed in place. Rather, the political culture may change over time, sometimes slowly and sometimes rapidly depending on the circumstances. Clearly Spanish and Portuguese political culture today is quite different from what it was historically or even thirty years ago. It is more open, more democratic, less religious, more liberal, more secular, more modern and European. Does that mean that Spain and Portugal have definitely left their authoritarian pasts behind and consolidated pluralism and democracy? It could be. But while the recent changes in Iberian political culture have been impressive, there are also many continuities with the past. That is why we need to examine the political culture carefully, because it provides *one* of the key indicators as to whether or not Spain and Portugal have successfully bridged the transition to democracy.

Historic Political Culture

Spain and Portugal are old societies, old cultures. Their known histories go back over two thousand years; the weight of this long history, the heavy hand of the past, still hangs ponderously over both countries—and their former colonies in Latin America.[5] During these two millennia they have been powerfully shaped by indigenous, Roman, Visigothic, Christian, and Islamic influences, as well as by more modern European trends including rock music, dress styles, and—not least—democracy. Here we analyze some of the historic elements of Iberian political culture; later in the chapter we talk about the change process.

Catholicism

Iberian Catholicism has long been more intolerant, more absolutist, and more fanatical than Catholicism in many other parts of Europe or in the United States. It was Spain, after all, that fought a long, five-century crusade against Islam and the Moors during the Middle Ages, established the brutal and repressive Inquisition to root out heretical ideas, drove out the Jews in 1492, and carried out the bloody—but ultimately unsuccessful—Counter-Reformation against rising Protestantism in the sixteenth and seventeenth centuries. Portuguese Catholicism has not usually been so absolutist, intolerant, and forceful as Spanish Catholicism, but it has been similarly monopolistic and authoritarian.

The main reason Spanish Catholicism has been so intolerant is that it has long felt threatened. It was threatened by the strength of Islam during the seven-century period of Moorish domination of Iberia; it felt threatened by and jealous of the power, money, and influence of the Jews in the late Middle Ages; and it felt threatened in the sixteenth century by Protestantism and the breaking of Catholic unity and monopoly in Europe. Hence, Spain took upon itself the role of defender of the faith, seeking to drive out and suppress what it regarded as heresies; it embarked on a new crusade that helped ruin Spain financially and drove out some of her most talented and able people. Since the French Revolution of 1789, the Spanish church has felt most threatened by liberalism, pluralism, and republicanism, and long took vigorous action to stamp out these more recent "heresies." Marxism and Bolshevism have also been anathema to the Spanish church.

The reason Iberian Catholicism is of so much interest to us here is that Catholicism was not only a body of religious beliefs, but it undergirded the educational system, the legal system, the pattern of social relations, and the political structure as well. The same religious beliefs that stressed order, discipline, hierarchy, and authority also provided the foundation for the political system. Catholicism was not just something that could be compartmentalized and confined to the religious sphere, as in the American doctrine of the separation of church and state; it infused legal, educational, social, political, even economic relations as well. All walks of life were informed by Catholic principles; the religious, social, and political spheres could not be separated. Spain and Portugal were not only Catholic countries in their religious beliefs, but they were also Catholic cultures, Catholic societies, and Catholic polities.

Now this is all changing. The Church is less influential in Spain. Vocations are down, attendance at Mass is down, and fewer Spaniards consider themselves Catholic. Even fewer participate in the sacraments regularly. As Spain and Portugal have modernized, they have also become more secularized, materialistic, and nonreligious. Hence, as the Church has become less powerful, the political-cultural values associated with it—conservatism, traditionalism, intolerance, and so on—have also declined in influence.

Authoritarianism

Authoritarianism has long been associated with Spanish and Portuguese political culture. Authoritarianism implies top-down rule, power emanating from above, and the absence of grass-roots participation and democracy. Authoritarianism often means dictatorship. Interestingly, authoritarianism in Spanish and Portuguese life is not just associated with the national political sphere; it also pervades the family (domination by the father), the educational system (knowledge imparted from on high), the workplace (domination by bosses), the social structure (elitism and inequality), and virtually *all* areas of life. Authoritarianism in Iberia is, thus, a general rather than a solely political phenomenon.

Authoritarianism in Spain and Portugal stems from the same medieval and traditional Catholic beliefs analyzed earlier. Historic Catholic political doctrine provided Christian legitimacy for a strong but just prince and the need for order, discipline, stability, and hierarchy. These are all profoundly conservative principles. "I need authority for my cattle," said one recent Portuguese politician out on the stump, "and I will need authority for my people." The crowd cheered. One cannot imagine a North American or North European audience expressing approval for such rank authoritarian sentiments. And recall that Franco was the *Caudillo de España* (the authoritarian man on horseback of Spain) *por la gracia de dios* (by the grace of God)—not by the grace of the majority or of democracy or one-person-one-vote.

If power emanates from God and is therefore, presumably, good, there is no reason to limit or check and balance it. Nor is there a need for elections, separation of powers, or a bill of rights. It is the ruler, as the chosen instrument of God, who grants all such rights. They are not inalienable or indivisible. The ruler may govern absolutely—may suspend all rights. He or she should not govern as a tyrant, but his or her authority remains strong. Nor, if the ruler's power and authority stems from God, should one resist that authority, let alone rebel against it. Authority is God-given and to rebel against it is to resist God, to rebel against His authority. If one is a serious Catholic, as most people in Spain and Portugal have been historically, one does not violate these injunctions lightly. For to do so is not only to tempt the ruler's wrath but God's wrath as well. For a believer, rebelling against God's Holy Word is inviting damnation. So given these ethical and religious imperatives, it is not hard to understand why the principles and institutions of authority have been so powerful and long-lasting in Iberia and why the resistance to that authority has most often been feeble.

Authoritarianism in Spain and Portugal stems not just from culture, but also from institutions—or, better, the lack thereof. Historically Spain and Portugal have long been characterized by the absence of institutional infrastructure—political parties, interest groups, neighborhood and community groups, civic associations, and associational life of all kinds—that is the essence of pluralist, grass-roots democracy. In the absence of such intermediaries, and given the centrifugal or "invertebrated" forces in Spanish and Portuguese society that have often torn these countries apart, strong, authoritarian leadership, it is reasoned, is what keeps these two countries from disintegrating. In more recent times (the Franco and Salazar eras), the need for a strong state has also grown out of the desire for rapid economic growth and central state planning. But now all this—and the political culture—is changing.

Elitism and Social Hierarchy

It is not just the rulers who receive their authority from God, but in the Spanish and Portuguese tradition the entire social hierarchy and class structure are ordained by God. The system is fixed and immutable, providing few opportunities for moving up the social scale. And once again, since this hierarchy is God-given, one should not, except in the most grievous of circumstances, rebel against it. Instead, one *accepts* one's station in life, for this is in accord with God's law and will. Rebelling against either a ruler or against those higher up in the social hierarchy is to risk violating God's law and invite the punishment that will surely follow, as well as eternal damnation. How old-fashioned, reactionary, or maybe just quaint this all sounds to modern, secular, non-Hispanic ears; but to understand Spain and Portugal we need to place ourselves in their people's shoes and to comprehend these societies on their terms, not ours.

The best way to understand the pervasive notion of elitism, inegalitarianism, and social hierarchy in Spain and Portugal is to go back to the Catholic foundations of Iberian life: St. Augustine, St. Thomas Aquinas, maybe Dante, and the Jesuit writers of the sixteenth century (Suárez, Soto, Vitoria, Molina). All of them have pictured society as organized on an authoritarian and hierarchical basis. At the top, as shown in Table 4.1, is God, from whom all power flows. Then come seraphim, cherubim, archangels, angels,

Table 4.1. The Spanish and Portuguese Societal Hierarchy*

God Seraphim Cherubim Archangels Angels Other heavenly beings	Heavenly beings
Kingdoms Principalities The nobility The clergy	The powers
Soldiers Artisans Craftsmen Merchants	The "old" middle class
Workers Peasants	Laboring classes
Gypsies Indians Blacks	Questionable if human or not
Lions Foxes Dolphins	The higher animals
Other animals and living and creeping things Trees and bushes	Other animals and living things
Rocks and "inert matter"	Nonliving things

*Adapted from Dante and St. Thomas Aquinas.

and other heavenly beings. (Those readers who attended catechism as children will understand this better than others; suddenly, those catechism classes that bored you as a youth will now help you in understanding Spain and Portugal.)

Eventually, in this social hierarchy, one gets to people; but only certain kinds of people. At the top come monarchs whose authority, like Franco claimed his to be, is derived from God's divine will for the universe. It is probably no coincidence that the political concept of "divine-right monarchy," which stood against the emerging principle of popular sovereignty, had its origins and strongest expression in Spain and Portugal. After the monarch comes the nobility, with its various ranks, whose authority, position, land, and peasants are also God-given. One can no more rebel against this level of authority than one can against princes. Next comes the "old" middle class, occupying an indeterminate and insecure rung on the social hierarchy: soldiers, artisans, craftsmen, merchants. Then come workers and peasants, who were obliged to work with their hands and to accept their station in life. Finally come the lower orders—African slaves, gypsies, eventually (in the New World) Indians—of whom it was not clear whether or not they had souls. And if they had no souls, they had no legal rights as even the lowest-class Spaniard or Portuguese possessed and could, therefore, be treated as animals whose higher orders (lions, foxes, dolphins) they approximated in the social hierarchy.

It is important to emphasize how fixed and immutable this hierarchy was. One was born into a certain station in life; one grew up in that station, married there, died there; one's children occupied the same station. Generation after generation and century after century the same social hierarchy, with only slight variations, was perpetuated. Spanish and Portuguese children would never grow up and hear, nor would they believe them if they did hear, the same Ben Franklin/Horatio Alger myths as their North American counterparts: work hard, save your money, study hard, get ahead. For the Spanish and Portuguese that was not possible. Life for them was unchanging, static, not improvable; one accepted one's station in life rather than trying to overcome it; the social hierarchy remained closed, and there were few if any upward escalators.

Family and Clan Groups

Spanish and Portuguese society has long been a society of clans and families. Some call them almost "tribal" in nature, a term that connects Iberia to Africa via the long Moorish occupation, and that doubtless carries the implication of an ethnic slur. Spain and Portugal are, of course, sensitive to these slurs and have sought to avoid them. But even today what passes for a "political party" or an "interest group" in Spain and Portugal are often really modern-day reincarnations, or sometimes disguises, for a family or a clan group.

When we speak of the continuing importance of the "family" in Spain and Portugal, we are referring to the extended family and not just the nuclear family. It includes brothers, sisters, uncles, aunts, cousins, and second cousins—and their children. It also includes ritual family members—godparents, godchildren, and their families. In addition, it may include political relations: members of one's graduating class (civilian or military); close friends and their families; persons linked to one over the years by employment, favors, patronage, or business deals. Such extended families may number several hundred or even thousand persons. They are held together by ties of blood, favors, trust, and mutual obligations.

Portugal was long dominated by seven or eight of these major families—or *grupos*. Spain, a larger and more complex society, has similar clans at both the regional and the national level. Typically, one of these elite clan groups will have diverse investments: a bank (both as a commercial venture and to handle the family's finances), a newspaper (to get the family's point of view across), a construction company (to take advantage of government public works projects), an insurance agency (to take advantage of compulsory insurance laws), a travel agency, a hotel and/or apartments, an office building, and land and cattle. Typically, too, the clan will have several of its members in each of the main political parties so that no matter which is in power, the family will be eligible for high government positions and will have its interests protected. Through its banks the clan may make loans to the government or help facilitate international financial transfers—a favor that, it is expected, would be returned with another favor.

Knowledge about these family and clan groups is limited. Unlike parties or interest groups that are studied much more because their activities are far more public, the clan groups are far more difficult for outsiders to penetrate. They often hide their activities, jealously guard their privacy, disguise their true nature behind other labels (if you scratch a political party in Spain or Portugal, it is often said, you discover one of these extended families), shield their members from scrutiny, block access to nonmembers, alter their surnames to hide their family connections, and close ranks around their own. This makes it very hard for outside investigators to understand them. Yet most close observers of Spanish and Portuguese society and politics are convinced these groups are very important, maybe even more so than the visible and public political parties and interest groups. Unless we understand these extended families, clans, and "tribes," we may be missing one of the most important institutions in Spanish and Portuguese life.

Patrimonialism

The phenomenon of patrimonialism is closely related to the family and clan network system just described. Patrimonialism refers to a society dominated by mutual obligation, by patronage, by gifts and favors granted in return for loyalty and service. In ancient Roman usage, a *patron* was a master or landowner who had freed his slaves but still had some rights over them—rights to a certain number of days of labor, for example, or to military service on behalf of the patron or, more recently, to support his candidates at election time. The patron is often a landowner and has seignorial, or quasi-feudal, rights over those who work on his estate—hence, the Spanish term *señor*, which is both a form of respectful address and an indication of the person's social importance. The patron has certain preeminent rights, but he also has the obligation to take care of those less fortunate than he. Just as God looks after His flock, so a patron must take care of those of lower rank in society: serving as godfather to their children, bailing them out of trouble, helping them along when the opportunity arises. Of course, the recipient of these favors is expected, when called upon or the opportunity arises, to return the favor.

A patrimonial society, in this sense, is one dominated by the granting of favors in return for favors, of obligations in return for obligations, in ways that can become quite complex and that may go on for generations. Patrimonialism has feudal and medieval origins deriving from the historic relationship between lord and peasant. Patrimonialism is usually pictured as a form of traditional authority in contrast to a modern society based on contract, mutual consent, and merit. But patrimonialism in Spain and Portugal, although having ancient origins, also has modern-day political expressions: a government job in return for a vote or other favor, a patron who carries his followers with him into office, political parties that mainly dispense patronage rather than standing for issues and ideology, a particular government office or interest group that is dominated by a single family clan, the hiving off of government programs so that they benefit not the general public but only a private or clan interest, and so on. Patronage has by no means disappeared as Spain and Portugal have modernized, but it now has to be exercised more discreetly; it is no longer the only coin of political power (elections and merit also count), and the patronage system itself has become more complex and "modern," centering no longer around land but on government jobs and programs.

Organicism and Corporatism

Organicism and corporatism stem from the self-same Christian, Catholic, and Thomistic origins as do so many other political-cultural features of

Spanish and Portuguese social and political life. When we say a society is "organic," we mean that it is unified, integral, closely tied together. All its parts are harmonized and in the proper relationship—as God has ordained in I Corinthians 13. Just as God designed His universe in perfect order, so the proper society must also have an integrated and proper plan. And just as God created men and women in His perfect image, so the body politic must also reflect the integrated unity of the human body, with its parts all interrelated, in perfect harmony, mutually interdependent, and so on. There is little room in such conception for political pluralism and the complex competitions for power and the separation of powers of democracy.

Corporatism in this conception refers to the several natural, integral, functional units that make up society: the family, the Church, the parish, the towns, the military, the bureaucracy, the university, and eventually organized business and labor. Earlier it was suggested that there was both an historic political-cultural sense of corporatism and a modern, political-institutional form. Under Franco and Salazar, Spain and Portugal sought to combine these two senses of corporatism, but here we are concerned with corporatism in its "natural" or political-cultural form.[6]

The corporate units that make up society are also to be organized in an integral and organic fashion, again corresponding to God's just ordering of the universe. The Church has its place in society, the army its place, labor its place, and so on. There is little room for change in such a conception, or for much overlapping membership, or for much competition and pluralism of ideas. Nor is there supposed to be "rebellion" (strikes by labor or lockouts by management) against this corporate system. Rather, society is supposed to be tied closely together into an organic whole with all its parts (individual as well as corporate) intermeshed in accord with God's just and harmonious ordering of the universe. In this way the organic and corporate conceptions of society are closely intertwined.

We now have in these preceding pages at least three ways of conceptualizing Spanish and Portuguese society. First, we have a system of social categories, rank orderings, and hierarchy—a system derived in part from history, political culture, and the writings of the Church fathers, but also created in part and certainly reinforced by an emerging structure of class relations. Second, we have the system of family and clan relations, dominated by patronage considerations and patrimonialism—a system in which various elite families and their retainers and clientele may compete for power and political spoils, and that overlaps with the social and class structure in various ways. And third, we have the system of corporations—a vertical structure that is distinct from the horizontal class-based one, but that also overlaps with the social hierarchy in various ways.

Figure 4.1 presents these three conceptions of society graphically. If we understand these three graphics and how the system that each depicts works, then we are a long way toward understanding Spanish and Portuguese politics. But now if we superimpose the three representations on top of each other, as in Figure 4.2, we can begin to envision Spanish and Portuguese politics in all their multifaceted complexity. If we then superimpose on top

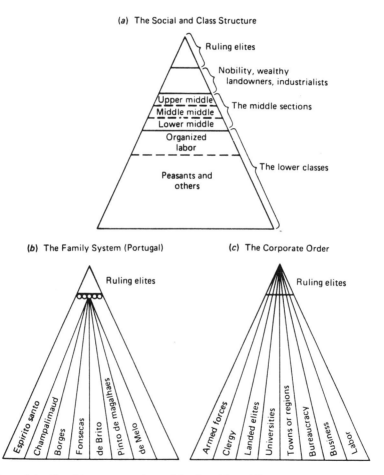

Figure 4.1   Graphic representations of the Spanish and Portuguese systems. Reprinted by permission from Howard J. Wiarda. *Politics in Iberia: The Political Systems of Spain and Portugal.* © 1993 by Howard J. Wiarda. Published by HarperCollins.

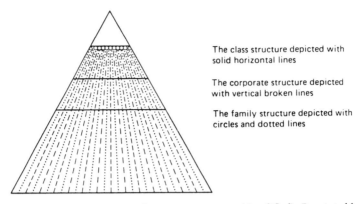

The class structure depicted with solid horizontal lines

The corporate structure depicted with vertical broken lines

The family structure depicted with circles and dotted lines

Figure 4.2   The class, family, and corporate structure (simplified). Reprinted by permission from Howard J. Wiarda. *Politics in Iberia: The Political Systems of Spain and Portugal.* © 1993 by Howard J. Wiarda. Published by HarperCollins.

of that a political party system, a modern interest group system, and a political or governmental system, we are *really* beginning to comprehend Spain and Portugal. But it is almost impossible to depict such a schema graphically and still make sense of it. If we cannot understand it all, we should not feel alone, for the Spanish and Portuguese cannot always comprehend it either—and they were born to the system.

A few illustrations may help provide a sense of the interrelatedness and complexity of the system. For example, those at the top of the social and economic class structure tend also to be the heads or "godfathers" of the main family or clan groups. They relate to those below them in the social scale not only by considerations of class rank but also by the system of patronal or godfather relations that are at the heart of the family network. By the same token, these family elites may dominate or be in control of one of the main corporate or interest groups, or one of the political parties, or have an influential family member in place there. They may now relate to those below them in the social scale no longer by ties of interpersonal patronage and mutual obligation but also by the new relations of impersonal employer-labor relations or as government program director to lower employee. An effective "player" in the political game seeks to mobilize as many of these resources—class standing, wealth, family connections, institutional position—as possible.

The system becomes more like a lattice, with various interconnecting parts, rather than the simpler, old-fashioned hierarchy. It consists of different conceptions of society pertaining to different historical and cultural epochs superimposed on each other in increasingly complex ways. Rather than functioning effectively, it now has so many interrelated parts that it may be prone to ineffectiveness and perhaps pulling apart. The contemporary Spanish and Portuguese political systems are all but impossible for coordinated management. But before we go too far with this tangent we need to know more how the systems got that way.

The "Two Spains"; the "Two Portugals"

The political-cultural features we have already emphasized—an older Catholicism, authoritarianism, elitism and social hierarchy, family and clan relations, patrimonialism, organicism and corporatism—are products of a more traditional Spain and Portugal. They grew out of a medieval and semi-feudal Spain and Portugal, out of the Reconquest and possibly from an even earlier (Roman, Islamic) history. These historic political-cultural traits have deeply and profoundly shaped the Spanish and Portuguese people, their social and political attitudes, and—just as important—what other people think about them. Some of these political-cultural traits are still alive and vibrant today; the degree of their being so is open to some dispute among scholars, although there can be no question of the importance of the issue for the survival of Spanish and Portuguese democracy.

But beginning in the eighteenth century, recall, a split occurred in the Spanish and Portuguese "soul" or political culture that made the issue more complicated. One part of Spain and Portugal (the traditional groups—Church, army, nobility—and the countryside) remained conservative, traditionalist, and grounded in the hierarchical, elitist, and authoritarian conceptions already described. But the other part (mainly urban and middle class) was infused with the new and more liberal spirit of the Enlightenment, was more rationalist in its thinking, and was outward and European-oriented rather than closed and inward-oriented.

This conflict was reflected in the controversy over some of the Bourbon monarchy's modernizing reforms in the eighteenth century, most of which the liberals supported and the conservatives opposed as "anti-Christian" or "anti-Spanish." It was reflected in the intense debate over the liberal Spanish constitution of 1812 and the long argument over constitutionalism that followed. It was reflected in the intermittent but bloody and hate-filled Carlist civil wars of the nineteenth century, which again pitted conservatives against liberals. And it was reflected in the polarized politics of the 1930s republic and in the bitter civil war of 1936–39, one of the nastiest, bloodiest, and most brutal conflicts of the twentieth century. In Portugal this same fundamental split between liberals and conservatives was present, even though its expressions were not quite so bloody.

From the eighteenth century onward, therefore, two Spains and two Portugals grew up. There now existed two political cultures, side by side. These two political cultures were like two gigantic "families," two parallel pillars of power, one conservative and the other liberal. Each had its own values, its own ways of behaving, its own society, eventually its own clubs and newspapers. The two parallel cultures touched each other from time to time but rarely associated or communicated. Rather, they were most often in conflict, competing to be the dominant force in their countries. The differences between them were not ameliorated or compromised over time; instead, they stood apart as two wholly distinct ways of life. It was a liberalism that the conservative side saw as anarchism, libertinage (liberty without restraints), and anti-Christian, and a conservatism that the liberal side saw as reactionary, antimodern, and antidemocratic, for which there could be no accommodation.

To complicate the situation more, during the early decades of the twentieth century, roughly 1900 through the 1930s, a third unsettling ingredient was added to this already simmering cauldron. The new force was Marxism, often in its revolutionary forms. Recall that Marxism in Spain and Portugal in these early years was not always of the parliamentary sort; rather, its dominant currents were radical, anarchist, syndicalist, Trotskyite, and Leninist. These movements did not generally believe in democracy but were often dedicated to revolutionary change and violence. Hence, there grew up in Spain and Portugal not just another social *cum* intellectual movement— another "family" often with *its* own clubs, newspapers, bars, and political parties—but one that again brooked no compromise with the other two. For radical Marxism in Spain and Portugal not only denounced conservatives as reactionary but also denounced liberals and republicans as "bourgeois."

Hence, by the 1930s we had no longer just two Spains and two Portugals, but *three* Spains and *three* Portugals. The one was so conservative as to be reactionary and traditionalist and saw the other two as evil, sinful, and anti-Christian. The liberal strain was similarly exclusivist, often anticlerical, and opting for the most advanced and radical forms of republicanism. The Marxist strain was antiliberal and antirepublican, and despised the other two. These three ideological currents or "families" in Spain and Portugal were so far apart as to rule out compromise; they represented wholly different ways of life that we can summarize as (1) feudal and medieval, (2) bourgeois and capitalist, and (3) socialist and revolutionary. In the Marxist formula these stages were supposed to follow successively upon one another, but in Spain and Portugal all three political cultures were present at once, approximately equal in strength, and with no inclinations toward compromise among them. Thus, even when civil war was not actually being waged between and among these three main ways of life (and several smaller currents), the *conditions* of endemic or potential civil war were always present.

Authoritarianism, Repression, and a Subject Political Culture

Both Franco and Salazar had plans to deal with this problem in their two countries—the problem of such deep divisions as to make Spain and Portugal all but ungovernable. Once again the parallels between these two regimes are quite remarkable.

Both Franco and Salazar moved to illegalize, wipe out, and completely eliminate the Marxist or radical "virus," as they called it. To that end Salazar and the preceding military regime that had named him prime minister took harsh measures in the late 1920s and early 1930s against the Marxist and communist "family." They illegalized the Marxist political parties and sent their leaders into exile or to jail; shut down their newspapers and printing shops; suppressed the Marxist labor and peasant movements; and killed, jailed, silenced, or exiled all opposition leaders. Franco had come to power through other means, in a civil war that was waged as a crusade against the Republican forces. Those who had not been eliminated in the civil war were killed, sent abroad, or imprisoned in the war's immediate aftermath. The first years of the Franco regime were quite brutal—far more so than those experienced in Portugal. However, for both Franco and Salazar, Marxism and socialism were not expressions of pluralism that needed to be accommodated; they were "alien" and "cancerous" forces that required elimination. Some Marxist and communist groups continued to exist in both countries, mostly underground; but as a main contender for power, Marxism and communism had largely been eliminated. The radical strain had been expunged from the body politic.

Liberals and republicans did not fare much better. In Spain many republicans were killed in the 1930s civil war or assassinated in its immediate aftermath. In both Spain and Portugal the liberal and republican political parties were illegalized, their trade unions were similarly illegalized and forced to reorganize as state-directed corporative agencies, and their leaders were jailed or forced into exile or underground. Franco and Salazar, in general, did not deal quite so harshly with the liberal current as with the Marxist one: the liberals were silenced but they did not necessarily have to face life imprisonment, permanent exile, or the firing squad. Instead, most of the liberal and republican politicians were allowed to return to their homes and their private pursuits; as long as they stayed silent, did not criticize Franco and Salazar, and kept out of politics, the regime largely left them alone.

With the two other main "families" and political cultures in Spain and Portugal now eliminated or silenced, Franco and Salazar moved to resurrect, revitalize, and give a monopoly to the more traditional political culture. The Franco and Salazar regimes did not try (as did Hitler and Mussolini) to invent a fully totalitarian ideology to stuff down the throats of their populations, but they did have distinct ideas or "mentalities" for which they stood. These ideas included a strong defense of traditional Catholicism, authoritarianism, conservatism, social hierarchy and the obligation to accept one's station in life, organicism and corporatism, and nationalism and the idea that Spain and Portugal represented a "third way," distinct from either liberalism or Bolshevism. All these ideas were at the heart of Spanish and Portuguese traditionalism and reaction.

The Franco and Salazar regimes used a variety of instruments to carry out this program. They employed censorship to blot out alternative views (those of the other two "families"). The corporative system was not only a way of organizing the new society but also a way to disseminate regime propaganda. The press, radio, and television were all controlled by the regime and published or broadcast only what it wanted. The single party machinery of both regimes was also used as an instrument of indoctrination. Virtually all national institutions were enlisted in this campaign to instill only one belief system, one political culture—the traditionalist one—in the Spanish and Portuguese populations, and to discredit or eliminate other points of view.

Especially important as an agency of this kind of conservative political socialization was the school system. Teachers were carefully screened, and efforts made to eliminate dissenters. Textbooks were infused with the political culture ideas that the Franco and Salazar regimes wished to disseminate. In these texts, the family and the Catholic Church were pictured as the primary units of society. Children were taught to obey their parents and all those in authority over them. The contrary notions of liberalism and Marxism were strongly attacked. Class conflict was criticized, and the class harmony of corporatism was praised. Liberalism was painted as bankrupt and contrary to Spanish and Portuguese values.[7]

Franco and Salazar were pictured as the saviors of their nations. The principle of authority was enshrined in all areas: the political as well as the social and familial. The "social peace" of the Franco and Salazar eras was much praised, as contrasted with the "anarchy" of republicanism. Catholicism and its values were vigorously taught in the public school system so that even public education was infused with religious education. In this way the Franco and Salazar regimes used the educational system to inculcate the belief that their values were the only legitimate national values and that all contrary beliefs were not only evil and immoral but also non-Spanish and non-Portuguese.

No one is quite sure how effective these socialization campaigns were in Spain and Portugal. Undoubtedly they were effective—for a time. For many years in the 1940s, 1950s, and 1960s Spain and Portugal had no really serious opposition movements that threatened the regime. There was a remarkable conformity, no mass rebellions occurred, and social peace reigned—more or less. Dissent was rare, and the Franco and Salazar regimes seemed to be sailing on. The effectiveness of this form of socialization seemed to be supported by the public opinion surveys of the late 1960s and early 1970s that showed the Spanish population as *even more* conservative than the regime itself.[8]

In these ways Spain and Portugal were progressively depoliticized. They became *subject* political cultures rather than informed, civic, or participatory ones.[9] The Spanish and Portuguese populations were demobilized from the frenetic and intensely politicized period of the 1910s into the 1930s. Along with the effort to infuse the two countries with the traditional values, apathy was used as a further instrument of depoliticization. Spain and Portugal were, in a sense, tucked in and put to sleep—told not to worry because Franco and Salazar would paternalistically take care of them. An effort was made to turn back the clock and restore the more traditional, peaceful, "sleepy" society of the nineteenth century—or even earlier. The traditional "Hapsburgian Model" had been resurrected in newer corporatist and authoritarian forms.

But eventually all the regime propaganda began to wear thin. Many Spaniards and Portuguese stopped listening. Or they didn't believe it anymore. Or they became bored. New ideas filtered in. The population had other things on their minds—living like Europeans, greater freedom, opportunities for travel and alternative points of view, eventually democracy. A new generation had grown up that didn't remember or care about the ideological wars of the 1930s. Spain and Portugal under Franco and Salazar had been gigantic catechism classes; "public" education there was like being in parochial school all one's life. Although many Spaniards and Portuguese stayed on the "straight and true" path, many others—as sometimes happens with catechumens—grew up, lost interest, joined trade unions or the illegal underground organizations, or migrated to the centers of "sin and iniquity" in the cities or abroad. It was like, on a national scale, the child in America who grows up in a small town, for many years has the shelter of the family and the local community, attends church or synagogue regularly and maybe even goes to a parochial school—and then goes to a far-off secular university where his or her beliefs are challenged for the first time, alternative points of view are presented, and new and maybe potentially subversive ideas begin to creep in.

On a national scale, that is what, in essence, happened in Spain and Portugal. After all the years of socialization in the regimes' values, their peoples eventually lost interest and wanted to listen to other drummers, other points of view. As that began to occur on a larger and larger scale, the Franco and Salazar regimes—themselves becoming old, boring, and dinosauric—lost their hold on public opinion and on the political culture. By the time the Salazar regime was overthrown and Franco died, a post-Salazar and post-Franco political culture had already begun to emerge.

Social Change and Culture Change

Eventually Spain and Portugal awakened from the torpor of the Franco and Salazar regimes. They again became, by the late 1960s–early 1970s, vibrant and alive. Once more they were becoming mobilized and politicized, but not always in accord with the wishes of their reigning regimes. They began to turn their backs on the official ideology of the Franco and Salazar regimes and to go off in new directions. A new political culture began to emerge, replacing or again standing alongside the older, official political culture of Franco and Salazar. What were the causes of this major shift, this "sea change" in political culture?

The first and most important cause was industrialization and the vast social changes to which it gave rise. In Spain the economic growth rate was about 7.3 percent per year in real terms between 1961 and 1973; in Portugal the growth rate during this same period was around 5 percent. In Spain in 1930, the percentage of the population employed in agriculture was about 50 percent; in Portugal it was 70 percent. But by the end of the 1960s (near the end of the Franco and Salazar eras) these figures had changed dramatically: only 30 percent agricultural in Spain and about 48 percent in Portugal.

Industrialization and rapid economic development from the 1950s through the 1970s dramatically changed the face—and the political culture—of Spain and Portugal. The shift from agriculture to industry led to rapid urbanization. In the cities, the new working class had access to television, movies, newspapers, radio, and ideas unavailable in the countryside. These new ideas and media helped change the way people think, altered their outlook on life, and made them more secular and nationalistic and less attracted to Catholicism and the older values.

Industrialization and economic development also led to vast social changes. The middle class doubled in size in both countries between the 1950s and the 1970s, and their outlook changed—toward modernization and democracy—as well. A new business-industrial class grew up that was more sophisticated, cosmopolitan, and European-oriented. The working class grew and so did working-class consciousness. In the urban areas also, a large *lumpenproletariat* of semi-employed and underemployed peddlers, cigarette vendors, and penny capitalists also saw the city lights for the first time. Along with the class changes, therefore, came a growing change in political ideas.

Another cause of change was emigration. So many Portuguese and Spaniards were leaving the countryside that the domestic job market could not absorb them all. Millions immigrated to England, Holland, Switzerland, France, West Germany, and Belgium where they took menial jobs as waiters, dishwashers, construction workers, and garbage collectors. Although their pay was low by North European standards, it was high by Iberian standards. Many of these workers, who lived abroad for extended periods and then returned to Spain and Portugal, brought back with them advanced ideas of trade unionism, social welfare, and democracy.

Another important influence was tourism. By the early 1970s over forty million tourists were visiting Spain annually. The number of tourists equaled the total population of Spain. The comportment of these tourists, their affluence, their lifestyles, and the freedom they enjoyed undoubtedly had a strong influence on Spanish values. Portugal had far fewer tourists than Spain, but eventually the broader European influence was felt there too.

The European influence was stronger than just tourism and emigration, however. By the early 1970s many more Spaniards and Portuguese had traveled in Europe, had business dealings there, went there on holidays, and kept abreast of European events. The desire to be or live like the other, developed Europeans was powerful. That meant not just European affluence but European democracy and freedom as well.

In both countries literacy rates and access to education also began to rise. As Spain and Portugal became more affluent in the 1960s and 1970s, their educational systems improved; a higher percentage of children went to school, they stayed in school for more years, and even some adult literacy programs began. Education expanded people's vistas, taught them new ideas, and made them more aware of the institutions around them. For the Franco and Salazar regimes, "a little education" proved ultimately to be dangerous and subversive.

Finally—and it is a vague thing—values just changed. The Franco and Salazar regimes got old and ran out of gas. People no longer felt passionately about them, one way or another. In earlier decades many had been either strongly in favor or strongly opposed, but later apathy and indifference had set in. As Franco and Salazar got older, infirm, and less full of vim and *machismo*, people realized that they would go soon too, that they were not immortal. Everyone was sitting around waiting for the Franco and Salazar regimes to pass from the scene, which they eventually did. But by the time they did disappear, the values and political culture of their peoples had already changed.

In the 1960s, the Franco and Salazar regimes had been portrayed as perhaps *permanently* authoritarian-corporate regimes. They had been seen by many observers as models of how to achieve economic change and social modernization without those being accompanied by value changes leading to democratization. But as we have seen here, that was not an accurate portrayal. In fact, the value changes—changes in the political culture—were also occurring concomitantly with socioeconomic changes. But for a long time, while Franco and Salazar were still alive, they were hidden, disguised, below the surface, not immediately visible. In fact, Spanish and Portuguese political culture had changed considerably in recent decades; those changes, however, became apparent only after the Salazar regime and Franco had passed from the scene.

A New Spain, A New Portugal?

Spain and Portugal have undoubtedly undergone major changes in recent decades, including changes in their political cultures. The key question is whether these changes have been sufficiently thorough that we can now say Spain and Portugal have become full, consolidated democracies and are safely in the democratic camp.

To begin, let us examine the changing nature of Iberian Catholicism. Spain and Portugal have long thought of themselves as Catholic societies, cultures, and countries—often more Catholic than the Vatican. Franco and Salazar, in part, resurrected the idea of a confessional state, and survey data from the 1960s and early 1970s show Spain and Portugal as more Catholic than other historically Catholic countries of Europe (Italy, France, Belgium) and roughly at the same level as Ireland.[10]

Whereas in the mid-1960s 80 percent of the Spaniards described themselves as practicing Catholics, by the mid-1980s the figure was below 30 percent. Fewer and fewer Spanish and Portuguese Catholics attended mass or participated in the sacraments. They have almost no contact with the Church. They may still want their children baptized in the Church, they prefer to be married in the Church, and they would like before dying to receive the last rites of the Church, but these "hatch'em, match'em, and dispatch'em" functions do not speak of a strong and powerful religious influence still able to shape, if not determine, the overall political culture. The Church in both countries has also experienced a decline in its institutional infrastructure—schools, hospitals, vocations. The Roman Catholic Church itself, since Vatican II, has also changed, becoming more liberal and open. Spain and Portugal, meanwhile, have become less religious, more secular, more indifferent toward the Church, and even atheist. Along with this decline in the Church's influence has also come a diminution in the strength of the values associated with historic Catholicism: unquestioned authority, social hierarchy, elitism, and political absolutism.

A second trend is that the Spanish and Portuguese have become strong supporters of democracy. By percentages that range from the low 80s to over 90 percent, overwhelmingly Spaniards and Portuguese have expressed a preference for liberal, democratic, representative rule. By the same token, the support for democracy's main alternatives, Marxism-Leninism and authoritarianism-corporatism, has dropped to less than 10 percent each.

These figures make democracy seem popular and secure, but there are some disturbing subthemes that make the prospects appear less rosy. First, if we ask Spaniards and Portuguese what they mean by democracy, the answer comes back as "strong government"—which seems to imply the still-present possibility of an authoritarian "out," particularly if there should be a crisis or the economy should go into a downturn. Second, although democracy in the abstract is strongly supported, support for what we think of as democracy's essential supporting institutions—such as labor unions and political parties—is very weak, in the neighborhood of 20 to 30 percent. Third, while expressing support for democracy, when asked which was the best government they had in the past twenty-five years, more than 50 percent of the Portuguese said that of Salazar/Caetano. Finally, in both countries in recent years, there has been a certain disillusionment with ("it hasn't delivered") and decline in support for democracy, but it is uncertain whether this reflects unhappiness with the particular government-of-the-moment or if it is a more fundamental disillusionment with democracy itself.

A fourth change in the political culture relates to the declining influence of *amiguismo* (friendship, personal ties), *caciquismo* ("bossism"), and patrimonialism (government by mutual favors). Increasingly, it is merit and achievement that count in Spain and Portugal—*along with* personal ties and friendships. As Spain and Portugal have become more *national* political regimes, the power of the local bosses has also declined.[11] In addition, the patrimonialist features that were dominant in earlier decades are no longer so strongly present; now real public policies (housing, education, health care) must be carried out *in addition to* finding a place on the public payroll for one's friends and cronies. All this means that change has taken place in these areas of historic political culture, but it is by no means complete.

Fifth, Spain and Portugal have become increasingly materialistic and consumer-goods-oriented. It used to be said in some quarters that Spain and Portugal were "different" because they were more spiritual, more humanistic, more artistic, more idealistic than their presumably crass, money-grubbing, and materialistic North American and North European counterparts. Some of this may still be true; Spain and Portugal may still be "different" in certain respects. But the evidence indicates that by now Spain and Portugal have become just as materialistic as the rest of the world. That may or may not be good, but it does show that in this area as in others Spanish and Portuguese political culture has become less distinctive.

Another area of change, sixth, is in gender roles. Spain and Portugal have been, historically, male-dominated societies. But now middle-class women are increasingly joining the professions, while lower-class women are working in the thousands of factories, often foreign-owned, that have been established in the past thirty years. Although politics is still male-dominated, some women have occupied cabinet, foreign ministry, and parliamentary positions—even the position of prime minister of Portugal for a brief time. Children have also become much more independent and have adopted a freer lifestyle. All these changes have given rise to a variety of problems that are familiar in other advanced industrial countries (rising rates of divorce, delinquency, absence of child care, breakup of the family, and so on) but that are new to Spain and Portugal. In these as in other areas, the institutions that supported the historic political culture, and hence the political culture itself, are undergoing fundamental transformation.

Seventh, Spaniards and Portuguese have shown a marked inclination toward moderation and centrism. This stands in stark contrast to the period of the Second Republic in Spain, when public opinion became polarized, the extremes gained ascendancy, and the country broke down into civil war. No one wants to repeat that experience again. Portugal, too, after its conservative-versus-republican conflicts earlier in the twentieth century and the extremism of the revolution in 1974–76, has similarly calmed down and become more centrist. The extremes have been repudiated electorally and moderate regimes are in control. Outside of the Spanish Basque area, today there are no significant political movements of either the extreme Left or the extreme Right. Once again, Spain and Portugal have become "just like us"; the radicals are out and moderation and centrism are in.

Finally, what may save Spain and Portugal is apathy. In neither country are people so passionate about politics as they were earlier. Party identification is down compared with the rest of Europe and so is the percentage of persons who vote. More and more Spaniards and Portuguese are concerned primarily with jobs, getting ahead, consumer goods, money, and affluent lifestyles. Their interest in the great political issues has waned. These attitude changes had been building for some time, but a qualitative change came in the mid-1980s. From 1975 to 1985 politics was at the center of Spanish and Portuguese preoccupations, but by the mid-1980s democracy had been more strongly consolidated and attention began to shift away from political concerns toward economic concerns. The apathy, declining party identification, and lower voter turnout may be worrisome for Iberian democracy in the long run, but in the short term the decline of passionate politics may have helped stabilize these two still somewhat uncertain democracies.

A good way of summarizing all these political-cultural changes is to say that Spain and Portugal have become more like Europe. That is, institutionally and in terms of their values, the two Iberian nations are closer to Europe than ever before. They are no longer "different," no longer "Third World," no longer "African" or "Latin American." At the same time, it must be remembered that Spain has a per capita income considerably lower than the rest of affluent Europe, and Portugal lags even farther behind. Furthermore, the process of "Europeanization"—in part because of these and other socioeconomic differences (levels of literacy, poverty, and so on), and in part because of political-cultural traits from the past—is still only partial, still incomplete.

So, Is Democracy Fully Consolidated?

There is no doubt that Spanish and Portuguese political culture is changing; the question is how broadly and how deeply. Spain and Portugal had a political culture strongly shaped by Roman, Islamic, and medieval Catholic precepts: authoritarian, hierarchical, elitist, organic, corporatist, patrimonialist. But a parallel liberal structure emerged in the eighteenth century and grew up in the nineteenth and twentieth centuries, and along with it a Marxist sector began to emerge as well. Recent socioeconomic change has begun to ameliorate the sharp divisions of the past and have led to a more moderate, middle-of-the-road, and democratic regime.

And yet there are worrisome aspects and conflicting cross-currents in Spanish and Portuguese political culture as well. The survey and other data often lead to conflicting conclusions. Estimates are that fully one-third or more of the population still supports the old values: discipline, order, hierarchy, authoritarianism. These values could easily be translated into support for a strong, nationalistic, conservative government. Recall that when

Spaniards and Portuguese say they prefer democracy, they mean by that strong, forceful government. In addition, Spaniards and Portuguese have strong anticapitalist sentiments, which means liberalism in the political sphere has not yet been translated into liberalism in the economic sphere. But many social scientists believe you can't have a liberal polity without having a liberal, open-market economy as well. And if you do not, conflict is liable to arise. Put together, these sentiments imply the still-present possibilities for a demagogue, a populist strongman, a statist and nationalist, like Juan Perón in Argentina, to come to power. Such an outcome does not seem imminent, but in times of economic trouble, social unraveling, or political instability, one could still see Spain or Portugal reaching for such a solution.

In addition, there are still powerful elements in Spain and Portugal—leftovers from the 1930s—who are antiliberal and antidemocratic. These groups are not just indifferent to democracy; they tend toward the values of fascism. They are not just conservative but reactionary and wholly traditionalist. These elements are not presently numerous but they could combine with the statist, nationalist, and strong-government advocates mentioned previously; recall that over 50 percent of the Portuguese population still think of the Salazar regime as the best government they have had in the past fifty years. Or they may enlist the decisive influence of the army on their side.

Many Spanish and Portuguese institutions have hardly been touched, and certainly not purged or reformed, by the democratizing changes following the Portuguese revolution and Franco's death. These institutions include the armed forces (still wary of civilian politicians and wanting to continue to play a "moderating" role), the bureaucracy (where the same persons who served Franco and Salazar are still often in control), the Church (now more moderate but still with strong right-wing elements), and the elite business community (which is still not fully reconciled to democracy). We are cheered by the expressed preference for democracy by over 80 percent of the population in both countries, but we should worry about the lack of support (20 to 30 percent) for what we think of as democracy's and pluralism's essential mediating institutions: political parties, labor unions, and peasant associations. We should also worry about some subcultures in Spain, such as in the Basque country, where well-armed and well-organized terrorists are plainly not reconciled to democracy. And finally, we should worry about the so-called success democrats in Spain and Portugal, who are inclined to support democracy in prosperous times but in a social or economic crisis could easily be persuaded to opt for other solutions.

Substantial changes have thus occurred in the political culture of Spain and Portugal (and in Latin America as well) since the 1950s, but these changes are still incomplete. The trend has been toward democracy and liberalism, but there are just enough uncertainties present that we cannot yet close the door definitively on other possibilities. In earlier writings,[12] this author has suggested that it has historically been dangerous for one part of Spain or one part of Portugal (currently the liberal part) to try to rule completely without the other part, as if the other part did not exist. In the past that uncompromising attitude has been a formula for conflict and civil war.

The author now thinks that there has been sufficient change in Iberian society and political culture that the prospect for severe conflict is unlikely. But this author still sees the need for an accommodation with the older Spain and the older Portugal. The old society and the old values cannot just be wished away. Hence, instead of their trying simply to imitate the parliamentarism of the rest of Europe, the Spanish and Portuguese could perhaps use a political formula that combines liberalism and democracy with the still-valued traits from their own historical and cultural traditions. Such a formula might imply strong presidential leadership à la de Gaulle in France, a form of Rousseauian democracy (free but organic), or perhaps a form of neocorporatism (as distinct from the older, discredited form). The precise nature of these compromises needs to be worked out by the Spaniards and Portuguese, but if democracy is to not only survive but thrive, some form of accommodation with the past is likely still necessary.

Notes

1. Clifford Geertz, *The Interpretation of Cultures* (New York: Basic Books, 1973), p. 312.

2. Edgar Schein, *Organizational Culture and Leadership* (San Francisco: Jossey-Bass, 1985), p. 9.

3. See Gabriel A. Almond and Sidney W. Verba, *The Civic Culture* (Princeton, N.J.: Princeton University Press, 1963); Gabriel A. Almond and Sydney W. Verba, *The Civic Culture Revisited: An Analytic Study* (Boston: Little, Brown, 1980); and Lucian W. Pye and Sidney W. Verba (eds.), *Political Culture and Political Development* (Princeton: Princeton University Press, 1965).

4. An excellent statement is Samuel H. Barnes, *Politics and Culture* (Ann Arbor: Center for Political Studies, Institute for Social Research, University of Michigan, 1988).

5. See especially the essays dealing with Spain and Portugal by Richard M. Morse in Howard J. Wiarda (ed.), *Politics and Social Change in Latin America: The Distinct Tradition* (Amherst: University of Massachusetts Press, 1982, rev. ed., Boulder, Colo.: Westview Press, 1992).

6. Ronald C. Newton, "Natural Corporatism and the Passing of Populism in Spanish America," in Frederick B. Pike and Thomas Stritch (eds.), *The New Corporatism: Social-Political Structures in the Iberian World* (Notre Dame: Notre Dame University Press, 1974), pp. 34–51.

7. The best study is by Richard M. Nuccio, "Socialization of Political Values: The Content of Official Education in Spain" (Ph.D. dissertation, Department of Political Science, University of Massachusetts, 1977).

8. See especially the early surveys by the Spanish polling agency FOESSA, *Estudios Sociológicos sobre la Situación Social de España* (Madrid: Euramerica, various years).

9. The distinctions are elaborated in Almond and Verba, *Civic Culture.*

10. José Ramón Montero Gibert, "Iglesia, Secularización y Comportamiento Político en España," REIS, 34 (1986: 131–59).

11. Richard Gunther, *Politics and Culture in Spain* (Ann Arbor: Center for Political Studies, Institute for Social Research, University of Michigan, 1988).

12. Howard J. Wiarda with Iêda Siqueira Wiarda, *The Transitions to Democracy in Spain and Portugal* (Lanham, Md.: University Press of America for the American Enterprise Institute for Public Policy Research, 1989).

Chapter 5

The New Spain and the New Latin America: Five Hundred Years and Running

In 1992 we celebrated the five hundredth anniversary of Columbus's discovery of America. Politically correct persons in both the United States and Latin America have referred to the events of 1492 as an "encounter" rather than a "discovery," but in Spain—because the terminology reflects on its accomplishments and glory—Columbus's exploration is still emphatically referred to as "The Discovery." And, there is no doubt that Columbus's epic voyage *did* vastly increase our knowledge, expand our vision, give rise to the field of cultural anthropology, mark the beginning of the Western world's contact with and domination over the non-West, stimulate European economic growth, and—along with the Protestant Reformation, the Renaissance, and the scientific and industrial revolutions—constitute one of the marking points of the modern world.

As often nowadays with great international events, the quincentennial has been overwhelmed by our domestic political debates. There were heated, overwrought charges of racism, genocide, colonialism, and exploitation. But by focusing on the issues that resonate in our own country, we miss the deeper significance of the quincentennial. For the fact is that a great deal is happening in European–Latin American and specifically Spanish–Latin American relations which has long-term implications and of which we ought to be aware. It would be a shame if the domestic quarrels and the rhetorical posturings of the groups with political axes to grind obscured these larger meanings.

This chapter appeared in the December 1991 issue and is reprinted with permission from *The World & I*, a publication of *The Washington Times Corporation*, copyright © 1991.

European Trends

European interest in Latin America has been increasing since the 1960s. This includes political as well as cultural and economic relations. The new ties between Europe and Latin America are the product of increasing European prosperity and desire to play a greater global role on the one hand, and of Latin America's efforts on the other to "diversify its dependence." In both areas the desire was to reduce the influence of the United States. In Madrid, the European Community has opened since 1985 a now sizable office devoted exclusively to advancing European–Latin American relations.

But one needs to distinguish further among the countries and their purposes. France, which has concentrated its efforts in Africa, views Latin America as part of the larger Third World. Great Britain under Margaret Thatcher focused on commercial ties, particularly with the Southern Cone countries. Sanctimonious Scandinavia, which has few concrete interests in Latin America, nevertheless used the region as a way to castigate American foreign policy. West Germany developed the most sophisticated policy, encompassing political, diplomatic, commercial, labor, and intellectual ties.

The European presence continued to grow in the 1970s, but it shrank in the 1980s. France concentrated on Francophone Africa, Great Britain cut back drastically its university-based Latin American studies programs, and Scandinavia eventually tired of kicking Ronald Reagan around. Among the Europeans, only West Germany maintained a strong interest in Latin America; but now the unification of Germany and Germany's focus on Central/Eastern Europe means that its interests in Latin America have declined as well.

That leaves Spain. In many ways Spain is the most interesting of the European countries in its relations with Latin America. Spain, after all, has over three hundred years of history in Latin America between 1492 and independence in the 1807–24 period—even longer in Cuba and Puerto Rico before it was deprived of those last colonies by the "upstart" United States in the war of 1898. On several occasions in the nineteenth century Spain sent warships to Latin American waters in efforts to recapture what it referred to as "lost colonies." But Spain lacked the military and economic might to back up its lofty ambitions with a serious policy of expansion.

Following the debacle of 1898, Spain went through an agonizing self-appraisal. Who are we as a nation, what is our purpose, are we part of the First World of developed nations or the Third World of underdeveloped ones? Out of this reappraisal came the notion of *hispanismo* or *hispanidad*, the concept that Iberia (including Portugal as well as Spain) and Latin America shared not only a common language, religion, culture, and colonial past but also a common future and political destiny.

For a long time *hispanismo* floundered both because Spain lacked the resources to implement the concept effectively and because Spaniards themselves disagreed as to what, precisely, it meant. In the 1920s and 1930s there were some exchanges of artists, orchestras, etc., between Spain and Latin America—and a great deal of romantic talk, particularly in Spain, about their shared destiny. But at the concrete economic, diplomatic, and strategic levels, little change occurred.

Francisco Franco, who ruled Spain from his triumph in the Civil War in 1939 until his death of natural causes in 1975, attempted to give *hispanismo* concrete form, through Spanish economic investment in Latin America, more cultural exchanges, and a flurry of diplomatic activity. Franco also politicized the concept by identifying his own regime's values as those appropriate for Latin America as well. Under Franco, *hispanismo* came to mean discipline, authority, hierarchy, Catholicism (in its most conservative expression), social peace (enforced from above), and a political system based on corporatism. To *be* Spanish or Latin American in this conception, one *had* to subscribe to the values Franco cherished. If one did not, then one could easily be denounced as non-Spanish, non-Hispanic, or anti-nationalist.

But by the 1960s the Franco view of *hispanismo* was being challenged not only in Latin America but in Spain itself. In Latin America, especially Mexico, the Franco conception was resented, even hated, by liberals, republicans of various stripes, and by the Left. Right-wing forces, in contrast, often admired the Franco idea and the structure of his authoritarian state; and during the heyday of military dictatorship in Latin America in the late 1960s and 1970s, a steady parade of Latin American authoritarians, civilian as well as military, visited Madrid. They wanted to know how Franco had done it: that is, how, contrary to all the development literature then current, had Franco achieved economic growth and social modernization but without that giving rise to hated liberalism and pluralism. *Hispanismo* thus resonated differentially in Latin America depending on one's political position.

In Spain the issue was no less complicated. To emphasize order, discipline, social peace, and Spain's "uniqueness" identified one as a Franco supporter. But by the early 1970s more and more Spaniards wanted nothing to do with that kind of *hispanismo*. They wanted to disown the tourist posters that proclaimed Spain as "different." Instead they wished to emphasize their "Europeanness" and to join the European Economic Community. But to speak of "Europe" in the context of the lingering Franco regime was a code word for democracy. Hence, the debate over *hispanismo* carried profound political implications for the future of Spain.

The Reagan Era

After Franco died in 1975, Spain began a process of transition to democracy. Actually, in terms of the political culture, social relations, and public opinion, the post-Franco era had begun while the aging *caudillo* was still alive. All that was necessary was for the politicians and the political parties to erect structures and put into practice that to which the Spanish population had already gravitated. This massive shift in the society and political culture prior to Franco's passing is what made the transition away from authoritarianism and to democracy so smooth.

The transition was first in the hands of the moderate Francoists like Carlos Arias, then as King Juan Carlos became more assertive it shifted to the center under Adolfo Suárez and Leopoldo Sotelo, and finally in 1982 the Spanish Socialist Workers Party (PSOE) under Felipe González won power. These shifts also signaled a major change in the Spanish notion of *hispanismo* and in foreign policy.

Rather than the authoritarian-corporatism of the Franco period, *hispanismo* now came to mean democracy and human rights. Moreover, as the Spanish transition became more strongly consolidated and institutionalized, Spaniards began to talk openly of exporting their model to the still-existing dictatorships of Latin America. One can even say that the Spanish experience with building democracy after Franco's death (along with the other Southern European transitions in Greece and Portugal) began a worldwide phenomenon that first encompassed Latin America and later came to include significant portions of Asia, Eastern Europe, the Soviet Union, and even some early stirrings in sub-Saharan Africa and the Middle East.

The first post-Franco concept of *hispanismo* was quite moderate and restrained, but once González and the PSOE took power it became more radical and anti-American. González was, after all, a socialist and he shared the European Left's common hostility to all things American and particularly to the Reagan administration, especially its policies in Central America. But within his own party González was a voice of restraint compared to the Marxist wing of the PSOE. For domestic political reasons González had turned over part of his government to this faction, which was especially strong at the highest levels of the Foreign Ministry and particularly in the Latin America bureau.

A steady stream of criticism was now directed at the United States, which was made the scapegoat for all of Latin America's ills. Foreign Minister Fernando Moran, who eventually had to be replaced because he was so far to the left of the government's own thinking, delivered a succession of stinging, bitter, and, ultimately, gratuitous criticisms of U.S. foreign policy. He blamed the United States for Latin America's underdevelopment for the past two hundred years, a silly statement that cannot stand up under historical examination, meanwhile conveniently absolving Spain from any responsibility for the previous three hundred. His lieutenants and cronies elsewhere in the government, the Party, the Institute of Ibero-American Cooperation (a government agency originally established to propagate Franco *Hispanismo*, but now rebaptized and reoriented) and the Foreign Ministry were even more vituperative. These were their ways of acting out their Marxism and of getting revenge for the defeat of 1898, for U.S. military and economic support of the Franco regime, and for Spain's historic resentments of the United States for being "materialistic" as well as successful. The criticisms of Central American policy were related to the debate occurring simultaneously over Spain's joining NATO and whether it would be fully accepted in the EEC.

Quieter Times

Some Spanish intellectuals, and a handful of foreign ministry officials, who were caught up in the same notion of "dependency theory" (blaming the United States for all their ills) as their Latin American counterparts, actually had the audacity to see Spain (and others) eventually supplanting the United States in Latin America. But over the course of the 1980s, González and the pragmatists prevailed. It made no sense for Spain, these officials recognized, to have relatively unimportant Central America issues poison its relations with the United States on more important matters. Foreign Minister Moran went too far even for the easy-going González and was removed from office, replaced by a more pragmatic and centrist official. With him out of office, on to more obscure (and harmless) foreign ministry postings went the cabal of leftists whom Moran had elevated.

Other, larger things were meanwhile happening in Spain that made the government surer of itself and less inclined to rhetorical posturing. On January 1, 1986, Spain formally entered the EEC—after years during which Europe had kept the country at arm's length or, particularly on the part of the French, had thrown boulders onto the track. Meanwhile, González had reversed his opposition to NATO and campaigned strongly (and successfully) for its approval in a plebiscite. The visceral opposition to Reagan and his administration that many Spaniards—and Europe in general—felt was ameliorated over time. González's successful continuation of the social pacts between labor and capital that had helped make the transition to democracy successful, as well as the truly phenomenal performance of the Spanish economy during most of the 1980s even under a Socialist government, also increased the country's self-confidence and made it less defensive in its dealings with the rest of the world. Spain's was now the ninth largest economy in the world measured by total GNP; to its successful *political* transition to democracy was added economic success and far greater affluence for far more Spaniards than the country had ever seen before.

Spain's relations with Latin America also settled down, became almost "normal." The "grand strategy" of supplanting or at least serving as a counterweight to U.S. influence in the area gave way to a soberer assessment. Spain has long preferred to think that, because of the long colonial tradition and the commonalities of language and culture, it intuitively *knows* Latin America. But in fact Spain lacks the resources—the university centers, the trained cadres, the investment capital, the aid funds, or the large diplomatic missions—to have a large and effective program in Latin America. Moreover, while Spain liked to picture itself as serving as a bridge between Latin America and Europe, most of the Latin American countries felt no need for such a bridge; they could carry out their own relations with Europe quite well, thank you, without Spanish intermediation. Finally, the notion that Spain could serve as "model" for Latin American democratization, and particularly the condescending, patronizing way many touring Spanish officials advanced their own example, offended Latin American sensitivities and led to resentments.

Spain's overall relations with Latin America began to change. While never renouncing the earlier, lofty goals of leadership contained in the updated version of *hispanismo* (democracy, human rights, Spain as a model), the actual policy became more pragmatic. An earlier study carried out by the author concluded that Spain, whatever its wishes, lacked the resources and institutions to play a leadership role in Latin America.[1] Nevertheless, all during the 1970s and 1980s and on into the 1990s Spain's economic investments in Latin America gradually, albeit quietly, increased, giving it a larger presence there. Its cultural exchanges with Latin America also increased. Its diplomatic missions were trained to be less arrogant and to stop referring to Latin Americans, condescendingly and with an element of racism, as persons from "the Indies." Spain's popular monarch as well as

Prime Minister González made several well-received trips to the area, and González proved to be a useful interlocutor at several stages in the Central American crisis. Spain organized beginning in the late 1980s a series of yearly inter-American summits but, except on U.S. policy toward Cuba, it refrained from anti-Americanism and a too-ambitious agenda. In short, Spain's policy toward Latin America settled down, became more mature and even institutionalized, and was more effective for being so.

1992 and the Future

Spain still lacks the resources to be a major or decisive actor in Latin America but it has over the past fifteen years become a significant one. As a middle-level developing power whose chief, and virtually only, foreign policy instrument is diplomacy, Spain's position in the area has gradually strengthened overall, and become more institutionalized. Spain's foreign policy in Latin America must be considered successful. It has also expanded its economic interests in the area.

Of course, there will always be ties of common language, culture, and political sociology between Spain and Latin America. For a long time Spain was content to rest its case on these historic ties without doing much concretely to back them up. What is new in Spanish–Latin American relations in recent years is the slow consolidation of the more concrete (diplomatic, economic) manifestations of interdependence that have given the historic and cultural ties real substance.

But now Spain and Latin America are both facing turning points that will strongly affect their futures. In addition to the quincentennial celebration, 1992 was also the year that Spain became fully integrated into the EEC. Spain wants to retain its special relationship with Latin America, but the EEC, fearful of unlimited Latin American immigration into a borderless Spain thus exacerbating Europe's already troubled immigration tensions, wants Spain to sever its Latin ties. The issue is complicated by Spain's own desires to be considered "fully European" for the first time and to reorient its economy more toward the richer EEC than toward poverty-stricken Latin America. This last factor may prove to be more important than any sentimental ties, even in their recent, more concrete manifestations, to Latin America.

Meanwhile, with the world dividing into trading blocs (Europe, Asia, North America), Latin America is also scrambling for cover. It would like to retain outlets for its products in Europe, whether directly or indirectly through Spain, while at the same time taking advantage of the North American market and the United States's offer of a hemispheric free-trade market. It would be nice if North America, Latin America, and Europe (particularly Spain) could remain united in a new triangular relationship based on democracy, human rights, and open, market, prosperous economies. But the forging of such ties will require some extraordinary diplomacy; in the meantime, both Spain and Latin America may be forced to make some wrenching choices—between the older, historic ties that bind and the newer economic ones that beckon.

Note

1. Howard J. Wiarda (ed.), *The Iberian–Latin American Connection* (Boulder, Colo.: Westview Press and the American Enterprise Institute, 1987).

Chapter 6

The Spanish-Portuguese Transition to Democracy: A New Model of State-Society Relations for Iberia and Latin America

The weight of tradition, of history, and of the past has long hung heavily over Iberia. Isolated, withdrawn, cut off from the main modernizing currents of Western Europe, Spain and Portugal remained locked into the structures of the sixteenth century. They failed to experience the Renaissance, the Enlightenment, the Protestant Reformation, the scientific revolution ushered in with Galileo and Newton, the movement toward representative government of Locke and others, and the capitalistic revolution leading to industrialism—all the major transformations that we associate with the making of the modern world. Instead, Iberia continued as closed, Catholic, traditionalist, mercantilist, absolutist, and authoritarian—all the traits associated with the "Hapsburgian Model." A shorthand way to describe this is to say that Spain and Portugal remained essentially feudal, medieval, and premodern.

It should not be surprising that Spain and Portugal would be established on this basis in the fifteenth and sixteenth centuries; those were, after all, the prevailing institutions of the time. What is remarkable is that they persisted so long. They lasted through the seventeenth and eighteenth centuries of Spanish and Portuguese decline, in partially attenuated form in the nineteenth century, and in updated form on into the Franco and Salazar regimes. Some of these traditional traits and institutions are still present in Spain and Portugal today.

Published in Howard J. Wiarda, *Politics in Iberia: The Political Systems of Spain and Portugal* (New York: HarperCollins, 1992).

In the late eighteenth century liberalism began to arise in Iberia, helping to produce in the nineteenth century the phenomenon of the "two Spains" and the "two Portugals"—two "nations," two "societies," wholly separate and apart, existing within the same national boundaries. It also produced almost continuous conflict and civil war between these two conceptions, which were not just ideological rivals but had their reflections in distinct sectors of Spanish and Portuguese society as well. Traditionalism was strong in the Church, the army, the landed class, and the countryside; liberalism was strong in the emerging middle class, among commercial interests, with the intellectuals, and in the cities. Between these two conceptions there could be no compromise in Spain and Portugal; they were always at each other's throats. Therefore, from the Spanish and Portuguese points of view, liberalism and republicanism, as exemplified by the Portuguese republic of 1910–26 and the Spanish republic of 1931–36, seemed not to work; they produced chiefly chaos, disintegration, excess, libertinage, crisis, and ultimately, revolution or bloody civil war. Liberalism, they reasoned, may work for Great Britain or the United States, but for Spain and Portugal something else was needed.

But if in the modern age traditionalism was no longer viable, liberalism did not work, and socialism was unacceptable, what else was left? That is the question Franco and Salazar sought to answer. On the one hand, but only to a certain extent, both these long-term authoritarians tried to remain true to the historic faith in traditionalism, Catholicism, and an ordered society. On the other, they recognized that Spain and Portugal needed to modernize, needed at a minimum to update their historic institutions. To Franco and Salazar, corporatism seemed for a time to provide the answer, a way out of their dilemma, a "third way." Corporatism seemed to be a means by which they could both retain their traditional authoritarianism and ordered structures while at the same time, in a modern sense, organize both labor and capital for integral national development. In other words, Franco and Salazar were traditionalists in some senses, seeking to preserve historic institutions and the sociopolitical status quo; but they were modernizers in other senses, unleashing powerful economic and modernizing forces that, ultimately, they could not control.[1]

Unfortunately for Spain and Portugal, corporatism did not work very well either. Franco ignored or abandoned it first and moved to a system of greater political pragmatism and economic liberalism that stimulated vast social and political changes which, over the long run, had the effect of undermining his regime. Portugal's corportist system, which had earlier been largely shunted aside, was overthrown in revolution in 1974. There had been advantages to the corporative systems of Franco and Salazar: centralized decision making, a disciplined and orderly society, preservation of historic national values. But the disadvantages—absence of participation, no popular choice, dictatorship, absence of civil liberties and freedom, secret police, censorship, isolation from Europe, dependence on one man, no democracy—came to greatly outweigh the advantages. Almost all Spaniards and Portuguese eventually recognized this, so when the end finally came for these two regimes in the mid-1970s, few lamented their passing.

Now Spain and Portugal have embarked on a democratic course. The transition to democracy made in both countries has been bold, impressive, and inspiring. Overcoming major structural and institutional obstacles as well as the uncertainty of beginning a new course, Spain and Portugal have made significant strides toward democracy. But given the sad and pathetic prior history of republicanism and liberalism in Iberia, we must naturally ask how firmly established are these new democracies? Will they last? How much has really changed? How firm is democracy's base, and what does that base consist of? Will Spain and Portugal revert in the future to some new form of authoritarianism? Are the recent changes permanent or merely cyclical, bound to lead later on to impatience and disillusionment with democracy and to new calls for the discipline and order of a military regime? That cyclical process, after all, has been the history of Spain and Portugal in the nineteenth and twentieth centuries.

In fact the changes in Iberia since the mid-1970s (actually since 1960, thus encompassing the last decade and a half of the Franco and Salazar/Caetano regimes) have been little short of phenomenal. Literacy has risen dramatically, the pace of urbanization has quickened, and vast social changes leading to modernization are under way. The middle class is far larger and more secure, the trade unions are better organized and are recognized as legitimate political participants, and business and industry are well established. Spain and Portugal have joined NATO and the EC; their webs of international connections are far stronger than before, and the traditional isolation has broken down. Economic growth has been over the long term close to "miraculous"; affluence has increased and spread, some of it has even trickled down; and Spain and Portugal have been caught up in the world culture of consumerism, pragmatism, materialism, secularism, and changed morality. The changes in both countries are so great as to render them all but unrecognizable from thirty years ago. The changes also provide a much firmer social and institutional base for democracy than was true the previous times these two countries tried republicanism.

Although democracy is clearly being consolidated, pockets of resistance to it remain. These include elements within the Church, the army, the *Guardia* (Guard), and the economic elites. Many Spanish and Portuguese peasants are not enamored of democracy; the countryside is still more traditional than the cities. Nor have the police, the bureaucracy, and the judiciary changed greatly since democracy was established; and in times of political or economic troubles the new middle class could conceivably feel threatened and consider an alternative solution.

But note that we spoke of "elements" within these groups, not the entire institution or social sector. It is clear that in Spain and Portugal today those historic institutions that constitute the traditional triumvirate of power— Church, army, oligarchy—have also undergone vast changes, have accepted democracy for the most part, and are no longer automatically or necessarily hostile to it. Note also that we spoke of "pockets" of resistance, no longer fully half of a society or a culture of resistance. In Spain and Portugal not only have new groups and social forces risen up and been incorporated into the system, but the old groups have changed fundamentally as well.

In some of this author's earlier writings, he cautioned newly democratic Spain and Portugal to be careful not to go too far, not to antagonize the "other Spain" or the "other Portugal" or to try to rule entirely without it. In the past, that has been a formula for conflict, disaster, and civil war; and in the 1970s such cautions were probably appropriate. But by the 1990s conditions in both countries have changed sufficiently that the earlier warnings can probably be withdrawn. There is no longer a "second Spain" or a "second Portugal" (conservative, traditionalist, antidemocratic) capable of mobilizing sufficient support to overthrow democracy. The split that goes back to the eighteenth century, under the impact of vast economic development and massive sociopolitical modernization, has largely been erased. There are divisions in Spain and Portugal but no longer of that older type capable of tearing these countries apart. The historic division in the Spanish and Portuguese soul that dominated so much of the nineteenth- and early twentieth-century history has been mended—or, if not mended, then ameliorated, erased, or patched over so that it is no longer as troublesome. Spain and Portugal may still divide over newer class and political issues, but the older ruptures no longer seem dangerous or so disruptive.

We are now in a position to begin answering the questions posed earlier that have always been so difficult for Spain and Portugal. In terms of the historic conflict between traditionalism and modernity, for example, it now appears that modernity has finally triumphed, definitively so. It is no longer an even battle between these two, as it was in the 1920s and 1930s; rather, the social, cultural, and economic changes since then have tilted the balance away from traditionalism to modernity. It took some forty years, but the developmental accomplishments have been major.

In terms of the conflict between the democratic and the authoritarian traditions that have long vied for power in Spain and Portugal on almost equal terms, it now appears that we have an answer to that issue too. Democracy has triumphed. Eighty-five percent of all Spaniards and Portuguese favor democracy over any other system. Almost no one stands for or favors authoritarianism anymore. Authoritarianism has been discredited and largely routed. There are still *pockets* of authoritarianism in Spain and Portugal but no longer a whole culture of authoritarianism, a whole way of life encompassing vast sectors of the population. At the same time, although democracy has triumphed, the institutions of democracy—political parties, interest groups and pluralism, parliament—are not so firmly established and legitimated as we would like. Nevertheless, in overall terms democracy has been strongly established, and a strong democratic political culture has come into existence.

A third question is whether Spain and Portugal are now closer to the First World of modern, industrial, capitalistic nations or to the Third World of poor, underdeveloped ones. The answer is again clear, and it is not necessarily the answer that would have been given twenty-five or thirty years ago. Iberia is now First World: modern, industrial, capitalistic. A few short decades ago, mired in poverty and backwardness, Spain and Portugal might have been closer to the Third World—and sometimes, as in the Portuguese revolution of 1974, the ideology and feeling of belonging to the Third World came out publicly. But with the economic, social, and political progress of recent years, Spain and Portugal have become First World—and, again, definitively so.

In the past, the answers that outside scholars provided to the question of whether Iberia was First versus Third World, developed versus underdeveloped, often depended on their research perspectives and backgrounds. Scholars who studied Spain and Portugal after studying Latin America, particularly those who studied the Franco and Salazar regimes, found such striking parallels and affinities that they often interpreted Iberia through Latin American eyes, saw Spain and Portugal as only slightly more developed nations than those they had studied in Latin America, and tended to consider them together as part of a common Iberic-Latin cultural and sociopolitical area. Spain and Portugal as well as Latin America, in this view, were part of the Third World.[2] In contrast, those who studied Spain and Portugal after first working in Europe or from a European perspective tended to see Iberia as a part of the First World—a less-developed part, to be sure, but still European and not Third World. This latter interpretation, it should be said, is how most Spaniards and Portuguese preferred to see themselves, especially toward the end of the Franco and Salazar regimes—as "European" and not "Latin American."

In actuality, these differing views and interpretations reflected the fact that for a long time Spain and Portugal were located, on a variety of indices, between the First and Third Worlds. Spain is now classified as an "industrial market" economy by the World Bank, but it falls at the lowest rung in that category and even today its per capita income is only half to two-thirds that of such wealthier European nations as Sweden, Norway, and Switzerland. Portugal is at the uppermost reaches of the "developing nations" category, although its recent economic spurt may well have vaulted it over the barrier into the "developed nation" category. In short, our ambivalence about how to classify and interpret Spain and Portugal reflected the real-life facts that the two countries themselves were uncertain about their preferences and destinies and that the developmental indices used cast them as "transitional" or "in between."

At this stage the option of First World versus Third World in Iberia is no longer open. By all the objective economic criteria Spain has made it into the First World and Portugal nearly so. In addition, and even predating their joining the EEC, Spain's and Portugal's trade and commerce were so heavily oriented toward Europe that realistically, by the 1960s, they no longer had the luxury of choosing which bloc they wished to be associated with. They were already by that time European and First World whether they wished to be or not. Now, of course, these economic ties have been strongly reinforced by cultural (European), political (Western democracies), and strategic (NATO) ties. It is likely at this stage that these ties are unbreakable and irreversible.

The changes in both countries in the past twenty years have been enormous. These include impressive economic development, vast social modernization, and political democratization. However, in concentrating on these developmental parallels between the two Iberian nations, we should not neglect the considerable differences that still exist between them. Spain has a per capita income nearly *twice* that of Portugal and a gross national production eight times as large. Literacy is higher in Spain and, by all indices, social modernization has proceeded farther. In addition, Spain's social, political, and economic institutions are considerably more developed than Portugal's.

Hence, it should not surprise us that Spanish democracy also seems firmer than the Portuguese, on a more solid base, and better consolidated. Democracy in Spain, therefore, seems to be firmly in place, quite well entrenched, and with only small pockets of opposition. Portugal's democracy is also solid, particularly after the political stability and economic boom of the late 1980s, but its institutional and social base is still weaker than Spain's and therefore could, conceivably, be upset. At present that seems unlikely to happen, and I am not suggesting that such a democratic reversal is being predicted, let alone that it would be desirable. In fact, such a democratic reversal *in either country* would be a disaster—for the country affected, first of all; for Europe, which now has a big stake in Iberia's success; and for the United States, which has also strongly supported Spain's and Portugal's democratization. Looking at the two countries comparatively, however, Spain's future appears to be assuredly democratic; Portugal will *most likely* remain in the democratic camp, but its position is still a little more uncertain.

The accomplishments of Spain and Portugal in the economic sphere in the past thirty years and in the political sphere during the past twenty are little short of miraculous. They are all the more remarkable for having received so little worldwide attention. Spain has moved from an underdeveloped to an advanced industrial economy; Portugal is just about to, or may have already crossed the threshold into the developed category. Politically, both countries have successfully moved from authoritarianism to democracy. These are most impressive accomplishments, and they deserve far more attention than they have so far received. These are not easy tasks, and the number of countries that have successfully made these transitions is very small. The changes in Iberia rank with the transformations underway in the Soviet Union, the throwing off of communism in Eastern Europe, and the reunification of Germany as among the most significant events of the late twentieth century.

Although Spain and Portugal have indeed been transformed and in all areas of the national life, the continuities must be borne in mind as well. Even with all the changes toward a European system, Spain and Portugal remain in many ways distinctive. They approach and approximate the European political model, but they are not there yet; more than that, they retain—and are likely to continue to retain—particularly Iberian features and ways of doing things that are uniquely their own, products of their own histories and sociocultural traditions. They are no longer "different" in the way Franco and Salazar used to emphasize for their own political purposes, but they still often retain their own cultures, societal norms and institutions, and even political forms.

Spanish and Portuguese democracy, for example, still seems closer to the organic, unified view of Rousseau than to the Anglo-American conception of Locke. On another dimension, Spain and Portugal have jettisoned the authoritarian-corporatist institutions of their old dictatorships, but they still are organized, in part, on a corporative as well as a democratic basis. They are no longer corporative in an old-fashioned, quasi-medieval sense but, increasingly, in a modern or "neocorporative" sense in which both labor and employers are integrated into the state (such as through the "social pacts" the government worked out with the unions and business) in an effort to achieve harmonious national development.[3] There is room for further studies of how Spain and Portugal have gone not just from authoritarianism to democracy but from an older form of authoritarian-corporatism to a new and more advanced, more open form.

State-Society Relations in Iberia and Latin America; A New Balance and a New Model?

The balance in Spanish and Portuguese state-society relations has also been profoundly altered since the mid-1970s. What was once a strictly, even rigidly, centralized state and polity under Franco and Salazar has now been considerably decentralized and made more pluralistic. The authoritarian-autocratic Hapsburgian Model has now been replaced by a genuinely democratic one. With the rebirth of civic and associational life (parties, interest groups, regional organizations, and the like), coupled with the system of limited government and checks and balances found in the constitution, the societal component of the state-society equation has been enormously strengthened and the state component constrained. That is, after all, what pluralist democracy is all about; its firm establishment in Spain and Portugal in so short a time is nothing short of breathtaking.

Although Spain and Portugal are now democracies, they may still represent a unique form of democracy. The subject area is worthy of further research. It is striking how many of Spain's and Portugal's state-society arenas are dominated by special charters or organic laws that have the power of nearly constitutional basic laws. These compacts provide for a polity that is not completely unfettered or *laissez-faire* as in the United States, but one still dominated by provisions of mutual rights and obligations that owe a great deal to earlier Spanish and Portuguese history.

Such compacts between the state and its component societal units have their roots in medieval Spain and Portugal and in the efforts to strike a balance between the emerging central government and the autonomy of local and corporate units. Now, as then, there are organic laws governing the relationship between the Catholic Church and the state, the armed forces and the state, and so on. But these compacts also respond to contemporary political and economic requirements. In the modern era, of course, there must also be a charter governing the relations between political parties and the state, another for labor and the state, and so on. For virtually every group there is a separate organic law or contract spelling out the rights and obligations of that group with regard to the state.

In the case of Spain, this system of organic laws includes not just the relations of the state to functional corporate units but incorporates the relations of the central state to various regional governments as well. There has, of course, long been conflict in Spain between the centralizing aspirations of the national government in Madrid and the independent sentiments of the regions. Over the centuries this conflict has waxed and waned and sometimes been violent, as reflected even now in the movement for Basque separatism. But in the Spanish Constitution of 1977 provision was made to reconcile these historic differences. As with the relations between the state and Spain's component corporate groups, charters or compacts have been negotiated between the central state and the regional entities. These contracts spell out the respective powers of the central government and the regions; moreover, each charter varies somewhat in the relative autonomy it gives to each region. Spain has, in effect, become a federal system but it has done so using uniquely Spanish institutions. Portugal is less regionally oriented, but it has a relationship of semi-autonomy to the Azores Islands that is comparable to Madrid's relations with its regional governments.

In this way Spain and Portugal have sought to blend their ancient traditions of group and regional *fueros* ("rights"; *foros* in Portuguese) with the modern constitutional provisions of parliamentary democracy. It is a fascinating blend and combination—one that may make Spanish and Portuguese democracy unique, for what Spain and Portugal appear to have done successfully (and this is very unusual in the world) is to blend their own historic traditions and meanings of democracy with a modern European parliamentary form in ways that are distinctively Iberian. For want of a better name, we can call this a "compact" or a "contract" state.

If Spain and Portugal have, in fact, succeeded in blending European democracy with their own indigenous tradition of rights in a satisfactory, working relationship, then that is not only a major accomplishment worthy of far greater study than it has so far received, but it may have significant implications, as a new and innovative model, for the field of study known as comparative politics. On both a theoretical and a practical level, it may also have major implications for Latin America and other countries, cast in the Hispanic mold, that are similarly searching for ways to blend Western democracy with their own indigenous traditions and institutions.

Spain, particularly, and Portugal, in a less explicit way, have resurrected this ancient system of Iberian "democracy" while at the same time creating all the institutions (parliament, parties, elections, and so on) of a Western and European form of democracy, and managing to blend and reconcile the two. In other words, Spain has both an imported form of democracy that it has taken from Western Europe and one with home-grown or indigenous roots, both of which seem to be working rather well. Again, further study of these institutions and practices is required. But if it is true that Spain has successfully blended "outside" and "inside" forms of democracy, then that is not only a great accomplishment; it also has enormous implications for other nations of the world. Many of these nations, especially in the Third World and particularly in Latin America, have also been trying—most often unsuccessfully—to achieve the same blend, to take what is best from the Western tradition (democracy) and fuse it with native, indigenous forms and ways of doing things. If Spain and Portugal can manage such a fusion successfully, then they will have provided not only a remarkable case of development and democratization, but they will perhaps also have formed a model that other nations may wish to imitate.[4]

Notes

1. The details are provided in Howard J. Wiarda, *Corporatism and Development: The Portuguese Experience* (Amherst: University of Massachusetts, 1977).

2. See Kalman H. Silvert's analysis of what he calls the "Mediterranean Ethos," in "The Costs of Anti-Nationalism: Argentina," in Silvert (ed.), *Expectant Peoples: Nationalism and Development* (New York: Vintage, 1967); also Laurence S. Graham, "Latin America: Illusion or Reality? A Case for a New Analytic Framework for the Region," in Howard J. Wiarda (ed.), *Politics and Social Change in Latin America: The Distinct Tradition* (Amherst: University of Massachusetts, 1983; revised edition, Boulder, Colo.: Westview Press, 1992); and Wiarda, "Toward a Framework for the Study of Political Change in the Iberic-Latin Tradition: The Corporative Model," *World Politics* XXV (January 1973): 206–35.

3. Martin O. Heisler, *Politics in Europe: The Corporatist Polity Model* (New York: McKay, 1974); Suzanne Berger (ed.), *Organizing Interests in Western Europe: Pluralism, Corporatism, and the Transformation of Politics* (New York: Cambridge University Press, 1981).

4. For some broader comments on the Third World's quest for a model incorporating the best of Western and indigenous practices, see A. H. Somjee, *Parallels and Actuals of Political Development* (London: Macmillan, 1986); and Howard J. Wiarda, *Ethnocentrism in Foreign Policy: Can We Understand the Third World?* (Washington, D.C.: American Enterprise Institute for Public Policy Research, 1985).

Chapter 7

Transitions to Democracy in Comparative Perspective: Lessons of Iberia and Latin America for Russia and Eastern Europe

Let me begin by saying that we all have to be heartened by the enormously important transitions to democracy that have occurred recently in various parts of the world. In East Asia, we've seen some remarkable, although partial, transitions to democratic rule. In Latin America, we're now dealing with a situation in which nineteen of the twenty countries are governed by more-or-less democratic regimes—a stark contrast as compared with what existed twenty years ago, when seventeen countries were under authoritarian rule. There's been an enormously heartening transition in Southern Europe, by which we mean Greece, Portugal, and Spain. There are democratic openings and rumblings in North Africa and in some other parts of the Islamic world, and signs of openings in several sub-Saharan African states. And now we have all the changes in the Soviet Union and Eastern Europe! I'd like to draw on my own research experiences with this process in East Asia, Latin America, and Mediterranean Europe and develop some comparative perspectives about this question of transitions to democracy as it relates to Eastern Europe. (See Wiarda, *The Democratic Revolution in Latin America*, Holmes and Meier, 1990; and *Transitions to Democracy in Spain and Portugal*, University Press of America, 1989).

It may well be that for these purposes the Southern European context is the most appropriate comparative frame of reference, because Southern

Based on the transcript of an informal oral presentation by Dr. Wiarda at the Peace and World Security Studies Conference. Published in *PAWSS Perspectives* I, No. 2 (December 1990).

Europe and Eastern Europe are historically the two most peripheral and isolated areas of Europe, which means that lots of the new literature about dependency relations and center-periphery relations come into play. Eastern Europe and Southern Europe are also historically the most under-developed areas of Europe, the most lacking in long-term political stability and viable institutions, and perhaps the closest in various socioeconomic indices. And so I will try to raise some comparative perspectives about political transitions principally in these areas.

Let me first talk about the intellectual agenda for a moment. The first thing to note is that the literature on transitions to democracy, especially on the transition from Marxism-Leninism to democracy, is very limited. There's almost no literature at all. John Herz has a very nice little book, *From Dictatorship to Democracy* (Greenwood, 1982), which deals almost exclusively with the Nazi regime in Germany and with Japan and Italy right after World War II. That, unfortunately, doesn't help us too much in the cases we're looking at. Enrique Baloyra has a book, *Comparing New Democracies* (Westview, 1980), on transitions in the Mediterranean democracies that is quite useful. There's a very good book that the research branch of the State Department turned out, called *Authoritarian Regimes in Transition*, edited by Hans Binnendijk (Department of State, 1987). And probably the largest, although I think quite unsatisfactory effort, is the study by O'Donnell, Schmitter, and Whitehead on *Transitions from Authoritarian Rule* (Johns Hopkins, 1986). So the literature is very thin, although it's growing. We don't really have much in the way of conceptual road maps for this question of the transitions from authoritarianism to democracy, and I'd like to suggest that the road maps for dealing with transitions from Marxist-Leninist to post-communist regimes are virtually nonexistent. We have quite a bit of literature dealing with transitions from authoritarian and right-wing regimes to democracy, but not on transitions in Marxist-Leninist regimes.

Part of the reason for that, I think, is that our whole intellectual apparatus, which extends from the totalitarianism literature of the 1950s (Arendt, *The Origins of Totalitarianism*, 1951; Friedrich and Brzezinski, *Totalitarian Dictatorship and Autocracy*, 1962) to Jeane Kirkpatrick's formulations on these themes ("Dictatorships and Double Standards," *Commentary*, 1979) suggests that totalitarian regimes are unyielding, permanent, are in fact total (hence, the name), and therefore do not undergo such transitions. I'm suggesting that the mental equipment and models, going back to our graduate-student days, do not really equip us to deal with this question of transitions in Marxist-Leninist regimes. We also have to deal with the question of whether authoritarian regimes are in fact different from totalitarian regimes. I am thinking particularly about some of Juan Linz's analyses

("Spain: An Authoritarian Regime" in Allardt and Littunen, *Cleavages: Ideologies and Party Systems*, 1964) of the differences between totalitarianism and authoritarianism. One of the differences he analyzes has to do with the existence, in authoritarian regimes, of what he calls "limited pluralism," whereas in totalitarian regimes there is presumed to be no pluralism at all. My sense is that there are some very interesting differences here between Spain or Greece or Portugal in the 1970s, already quite pluralist even under authoritarianism, and the Eastern European countries and the Soviet Union in modern times, where the pluralism that did exist was much more restricted.

There's also the question of indigenous or home-grown models of democratic transitions. A lot of romantic talk has emerged in Eastern Europe and the former Soviet Union about the possibility of finding indigenous traditions on which a genuinely Russian or Eastern European model of democracy of some sort might be built. I think a lot of us have some sympathy toward that notion as an abstract possibility. In places where it's been tried, however, it's not worked very well. Our experience has been that when indigenous elites have tried to discover home-grown models of democracy and development, they haven't been very successful and their own peoples haven't taken to them very well. Western culture, whether we wish it or not—including materialism and consumerism as well as freedom—seems to represent what most people seem to want. It's rock music, blue jeans, and Coca-Cola that people desire and, along with these other cultural accoutrements, Western-style democracy, affluence, consumer goods, and human rights. Democracy is desired in the Western mold, not in some indigenous home-grown model like that tried in Tanzania or Zaire. My guess is that what we're most likely to see is some sort of mix of indigenous traditions and ways of doing things, which will continue to be present in Eastern Europe and Russia, along with imported forms and what Lucian Pye used to call "world cultural influences."

Now let me turn to the *setting* and *context* of these transitions, and try to advance a few comparisons that might be useful. The first comparison has to do with socioeconomic change. In Spain and Southern Europe, a great deal of prosperity and socioeconomic change had occurred in the 1960s and 1970s. Even before the formal political transformation took place when Franco died, Spain had, in the 1960s, doubled its per capita income, and then doubled it again in the 1970s. Portugal lagged somewhat, but its growth record was not all that far behind Spain's. What we are looking at, then, are societies in Southern Europe that had already become essentially middle class, urban, prosperous, and literate before the transition from authoritarianism to democracy occurred, and that's one important dimension and difference that we might want to keep in mind when comparing Eastern Europe and Russia.

Second, in the area of political culture, it's very clear that in Southern Europe, as well as in Latin America and in East Asia, there was a very powerful sense by the 1960s and 1970s that people no longer wished to be considered "different," as their historic authoritarian regimes had proclaimed and had always taken some pride in. The political culture had changed. There was widespread agreement, even before it took place, that the old regime had to go. Thus the post-Franco era in Spain, for example, began even while Franco was still alive, and, in fact, began long before Franco died in 1975. And these beliefs, in democratization and "Europeanization," were shared moreover by all sectors of the population. One didn't see the kind of split that one sees in Russia today, with deep-seated and quite polarized views about the future of the country. The surveys that we had for countries like Greece, Spain, and Portugal indicated that something like 80–83 percent of the population wanted liberal, representative, democratic, parliamentary rule even while their old regimes were still in power. That is, the political-cultural shift had already occurred even while authoritarianism was still formally in power.

Third, there occurred in all of these countries of Southern Europe an impressive resurrection of what we'll call "civil society," even while the old regime was still present. That means all the web of political institutions, labor groups, business groups, neighborhood associations, etc., that would be fundamental in constituting the nuclei for political democratization and pluralism later on. This is not to say that countries like Spain or Portugal under Franco and Salazar had become happy models of liberal, democratic, pluralistic rule even while their old elites were still in power. But it is to say that in the 1960s and early 1970s there was a remarkable political opening. The censorship, for almost all intents and purposes, was abolished. Political parties functioned not always as parties, but as "think tanks" or "study groups" in order to get around the laws prohibiting parties. Trade unions had been realistically recognized by the regime, and were no longer being so sorely repressed as in the early histories of these regimes. There was, in fact, a whole flowering, albeit still limited in the Linzian sense, of civil society, over about a fifteen- or twenty-year period, long before the authoritarian regimes themselves actually collapsed. And that's a very interesting factor one ought to think about in terms of its implications for Eastern Europe and Russia, where such trends have not been so strong.

A fourth factor in terms of the setting has to do with the international moment and forces. That is, the Cold War was of course still raging when Franco died, the Portuguese revolution occurred, and the Greek colonels left the scene. There was a very powerful role played in these processes by the United States, as well as by Western European actors. The West Germans, the British Labor Party, the Scandinavians, the socialists and social democrats of several countries, and the United States were all pouring enormous amounts of money into Spain, Greece, and Portugal, hoping to prevent what they termed the "Portuguese virus"—that is, a revolutionary transformation that might go in a Marxist-Leninist direction—from being spread to other countries in Western Europe. Everybody was involved: the CIA was involved; NATO was involved; the American Secretary of State was involved; the Socialist International was involved. There were high-level commitments by the United States government, by the West German government, by the British government, and by the Scandinavian governments, and by political parties and other private groups in these countries. The international involvement in Southern Europe to ensure that the transition ended up in a democratic outcome, and not in something else, was very powerful. My guess is that as the Cold War winds down, one of its unintended consequences will be less attention being paid by international actors—certainly by the United States—to events that are occurring in areas that we had previously thought of as Cold War battlefields. So Eastern Europe and Russia will not likely be the recipients of such large foreign assistance to assure democratic outcomes as were Spain and Portugal. Witness Romania.

Let me turn now from these general contextual characteristics regarding transition to democracy to a brief discussion specifically of political institutions. First, there's the armed forces. In Portugal it's useful to remember that it was younger officers within the military who led the movement for change, who got in the forefront of the revolutionary movement. In Latin America, in contrast, the armed forces were thoroughly discredited by their experience of government in the 1970s, and have largely retreated to the barracks. In East Asia, the armed forces have served as sort of moderative or tempering forces during these difficult and wrenching transitional periods, when things have the potential to get out of hand. And so we may want to think of different models besides full-fledged military authoritarianism on the one hand and strict civil/military separation on the other. We may need to keep in mind intermediary models where during the transition the military plays a limited kind of role in keeping a sense of balance and preventing change from getting out of hand.

Second, I'd like to consider social and political infrastructure. In thinking about this comparatively, I'm struck again by the fact that in all the countries where I've done research, in Southern Europe, Latin America, and East Asia, what has historically been called the *"falta de civilización,"* or the "vacuum of associability" in de Tocquevillian terms, had been largely filled by the time the authoritarian regimes left power. That is, if one looks at the sheer numbers of neighborhood associations, religious associations, professional organizations, teacher's associations, neighborhood groups, community action groups, and so forth, that had grown up in all of these countries in the 1960s and the 1970s, the changes are very impressive. If you know some of these countries, you know that the absence of associability has historically been the bane of their national political life, and in fact often called forth military interventions because there were few or no intermediary groups to serve as the basis of democracy or as a sort of brake on authoritarianism. Again, what is so striking about the other, earlier countries that have made transitions to democracy is that this vacuum of associability had been largely filled before the transition began. I'm not quite sure if that's the case in the Eastern European or Russian context, and this may be something we need to worry about.

Next, let us look at political parties. Again some very striking differences emerge here. I'm struck by the fact that in all of the successful democratizers, nascent political parties and groupings already existed at the time of the transition. They were already well-organized, albeit sometimes in exile or only partially enjoying legal or recognized standing. Some of them were aboveground and others were underground, but they all served as nuclei for the future political parties and party systems that would come into existence as soon as Franco or Salazar or the Greek colonels left power. There are several formulae that emerge from a comparative study of the role of political parties during the transition, but what's common to all of them—and the key, I believe—is a pre-existing party structure that was largely in place at the time that the transition began and therefore quickly flowered once the transition began. Obviously, the existence of these "pre-party" formations and an emerging party system made it much easier to complete the transition in an orderly way once the authoritarian structure was transformed.

Next, interest groups. Many of the same comments apply. I'm struck by the fact that in all of the successful transitions to democracy, business groups as well as fledgling (often more than that) labor unions were already in place and functioning within the existing structure and within the system of labor-employee relations. At the time, in all of the countries that have been successful in bridging the transition to democracy, we had also seen over a twenty- to thirty-year period an enormous growth of all the classic middle-class associations: associations of architects and engineers and doctors and professionals and so forth. All of these had emerged to form a solid and stable middle-class social base for the transition to democracy, which is probably lacking in Eastern Europe and Russia.

With regard to government institutions, much of the same kind of analysis applies. That is, there wasn't the necessity for a wholesale remaking of governmental institutions. Essentially what happened in Spain, Portugal, and our other cases is that the top of the political pyramid was lopped off. Franco died, Salazar died, Caetano was overthrown, the military juntas in Greece and Latin America were replaced. But the basic structure of government—the bureaucracy, the civil service, governmental institutions— remained pretty much in place both before and after the transition. There was no fundamental transformation at the governmental level until later when new constitutions were written. In all of these successful democratizing regimes, there was no toppling of the government (except in the Portuguese case), of the bureaucratic system. There was no need really for a wholesale bureaucratic housecleaning, which would likely have destroyed the expertise, the technical competence, that all of these regimes, even under their authoritarian rules, had been building up for twenty years. If one looks at the Spanish economic miracle of the 1950s and 1960s, one finds that it was led by a whole cadre of new, technically well-trained elites who eventually shoved Franco aside and almost into retirement long before he actually died. In contrast, Russia and Eastern Europe will probably require a thorough housecleaning of the older government personnel—with all the potential for conflict and upheaval this implies.

Finally, let us look at public opinion. In all of these countries we have some remarkable survey literature, predating the end of authoritarianism and during the transition. It's very clear that, with regard to public opinion in these countries, there already existed a remarkable consensus. It's striking that roughly 80 to 85 percent of the population favored Western, liberal, representative democracy. There was almost no sympathy in any of these transitional regimes for Marxist-Leninist systems, or for the major alternatives of corporatism or bureaucratic-authoritarianism. There may still be differences about what precisely is meant by these terms, but it's very clear that public opinion in countries that made the transition from authoritarian to democratic rule was overwhelmingly in favor of Western liberal democratic parliamentary rule even before the transition began. A similar consensus may be lacking in Russia and some Eastern European countries.

Now let me turn briefly to the matter of public policies. One of the things that comes through very clearly in the literature on transitions to democratic regimes is the importance of social and political pacts. Most of the successful transitions to democratic regimes both in East Asia and in Southern Europe succeeded in having business and labor brought together in a kind of neo-corporatist consensual agreement under government auspices, under which certain austerity measures were to be carried out in return for certain guarantees of social welfare, salary, pensions, and social security. What the pacts do, of course, is to avoid the polarization of labor-management conflict while the political transition—which is itself wrenching and difficult enough—is going on. A pact buys time, it buys space, and it buys social peace while other kinds of democratizing political change can take place. Russia and Eastern Europe are not yet at that stage.

With regard to economic development, the literature is strong in suggesting that it helps if a country can bridge the transition in a context of prosperity. That is, it helps if during the transition there is an expanding economic pie so that the older historic groups in the society can keep their shares while the new forces, the clamoring labor, peasant, and urban proletariat groups, can also claim their share of the pie from which they've been deprived for so long. In other words, it's enormously helpful if one can keep the old elites happy while also having new pieces of pie that one can give out to the emerging new groups. And that, in fact, was the case in East Asia and Southern Europe, where enormous economic development was going on concurrently with what one would have expected to be a difficult and divisive political transition. It's better in terms of democratic transitions to be rich than to be poor and to have a growing economy to cushion other blows.

On the other hand, we also have to recognize that in the Latin American context in the 1980s, the transitions to democracy occurred in a period of negative growth and enormous external debt. These countries faced a very difficult economic circumstance, and still succeeded in establishing democracy. So one would have to say that there's no necessary relationship between economic development and the capacity to successfully bridge the transition to democracy—but prosperity provides a solid base.

What about social policy? Again, what's striking about the successful Southern European cases of transition is the enormous growth of social programs in the 1960s and 1970s. Most of us grew up academically and intellectually with the fascism literature and phenomenon, and we view Spain and Portugal as fitting into that model. What we may have missed, if we haven't read very much about those countries over the past twenty to thirty years, is the enormous growth of social programs—education, health care, pensions, social security, housing, and so forth, which occurred in the 1960s and the 1970s, and which provided a stronger and better social safety net in which a political transition could take place. Now it's also possible, if we look again at the Latin American examples, that successful transitions to democracy can be carried out without this social safety net. But if that is the case, then the real crisis will likely come later on—in fact, is already occurring in many of the Latin American countries. And that crisis leads to a sort of post-totalitarian or post-authoritarian disillusionment with democracy.

Eastern Europe, including Russia, lacks this securer social and economic base.

It may be that we will have to add a fourth stage to the three that Pavel Machala outlined in his analysis at this conference. Democracy may not be the final outcome of this post-totalitarian process, but there may come, perhaps five or ten years afterward, an enormous disillusionment with democracy, because it has not delivered all of the socioeconomic goods that people have been led to expect. This may be particularly true in a context where expectations have been raised so high, which I think is the case in Eastern Europe and Russia. What made Spain, Portugal, and Greece successful as democratizers is the social programs that were already in place, and which provided a social safety net. In Latin America the social safety net wasn't there, but, on the other hand, expectations hadn't been raised so high. The real difficult case, it seems to me, will be the Eastern European one, where the social safety net is not as extensive as necessary and yet where expectations are very high. That's a prescription for conflict and polarization.

What about the role of foreign policy in all this? One of the interesting things that comes out of the Southern European and Latin American experiences is that while the transitions began generally as indigenous political movements, it proved sometimes very difficult to carry them out successfully without massive assistance from the outside. That implies extensive economic assistance, as well as political guidance. One of the striking things in the Spanish and Portuguese transitions, for example, is the way the European Community countries in a sense "took over" Spain and Portugal as their causes. They enveloped Spain and Portugal in so many EC and NATO committees and meetings that, for example, it gave the Spanish armed forces something to do instead of meddling in domestic politics. After all, who wouldn't rather go to Brussels or Paris on a paid assignment than muck around in domestic political affairs in Madrid or Lisbon? So, by enveloping the Spanish officer corps in NATO meetings, travel, and committees and exercises, they gave the military a new role, a function different from the historic role (which was to become involved in domestic politics). Mammoth European subsidies to these new EEC members also eased the transition.

This sort of indirect external influence was enormously helpful to the democratic transitions in both Spain and Portugal. Eventually, the socialist governments in both Spain and Portugal, which had initially been anti-NATO, recognized that was the kind of trade-off that they would have to engage in as a way of keeping the military off their backs domestically, so that they could carry out other programs that they really wanted to do. Staying in NATO was a way of neutralizing the Army politically. My guess is that, in the present circumstances in Eastern Europe, it will be Western Europe that can, must, and will lead in this regard. I doubt if the United States, once the initial flurry of interest is over, will provide the kind of sustained assistance over a long period of time that will enable Eastern Europe to successfully consolidate democracy. By its economic investment as well as proximity, only Western Europe can do that job. And Europe currently has other economic priorities and demands; no one can bail out Russia or Eastern Europe.

Let me conclude with a few observations. First, I'm struck by how little intellectual apparatus we have to deal with this issue. Not only do politicians not know very much how to bridge the transition from communism to democracy, but I don't think that scholars really have the intellectual apparatus, the terms, the concepts, to deal with it either. And I suspect a key reason for that is that our whole training in the literature of totalitarianism, and our understanding of the permanence of Marxism-Leninism, has not equipped us to deal with the fact that Marxism-Leninism can also undergo a transition to something else.

Second, in reviewing all of the cases, I'm struck by the enormous uncertainty of the transition process itself. There are, in Schmitter's words "numerous surprises and extraordinary uncertainty about the outcome of all of these processes" (*Transitions from Authoritarian Rule*). These are open-ended processes. Once an old regime unravels and old political institutions start coming apart, in the absence of widespread consensus of what the goals are, any one of many possible political outcomes is conceivable. And so we may have to live with a great deal of uncertainty about the future of Russia and Eastern Europe.

Third, I think that we have to recognize various gradations. We use the terms democracy and totalitarianism but there are many halfway houses. What we have to recognize is a whole set of categories or gradations within authoritarianism and totalitarianism on the one hand, and on the road to liberal, pluralist democracy on the other. In other words, our conceptual apparatus is once again faulty. We're going to have to recognize not just the dichotomous categories we've been using (democracy versus totalitarianism), but rather a whole set of types of regimes—mixed regimes, crazy-quilt patterns that blend authoritarian and democratic features within the same institutions and political systems.

Fourth, I'm struck by the enormous change that went on in the successful transitional or democratizing regimes of Southern Europe *before* they formally made the break away from authoritarianism. That is, we can see the importance of prior changes in the political culture. We saw enormous shifts in public opinion, and we saw major socioeconomic changes that had, in fact, created an urban middle class *before* the democratic transition began. I'm also struck by the degree to which nascently democratic parties, associations, interest groups, and even government institutions were already in place, however incompletely. When the democratic transition began, in other words, the successful democratizers were already part of the way there.

I'm also struck by the importance of labor-employer pacts. I'm convinced that one has to work out some sort of understanding or arrangement—if not a formal contract—between organized labor and workers on the one hand and employers on the other, with the state serving as mediator and guarantor, if the transition is going to be successful. If you have political transformation occurring at the same time that labor and capital are at each other's throats, with widespread strikes and labor violence, it's not very likely that your regime is going to successfully bridge the transition.

And that leads me to my final point, which is the importance of doing these things in sequence, to the extent possible. Obviously this is a social science construct and in the real world things aren't quite done that way; but it's striking, once again, the degree to which in the successful democratizers, socioeconomic change and change in the political culture had already occurred before the political transformation. That, I think, is critical: change can't occur all at once, but is better done gradually and in sequence. I don't think that Russia or Eastern Europe will have that luxury. It seems to me that in those countries we're looking at all of the transformations—political change, cultural change, socioeconomic transformation, international change—occurring at once. And frankly, I'm just not sure that a political system can handle all this without becoming overloaded. Russia under Gorbachev may be the best example.

On top of this, expectations have been raised very high in Eastern Europe and Russia, far higher than their political systems can actually deliver at this stage, facing economic crisis and in the absence of many economic resources. So my sense is that in some of these cases we may need a model that takes as its norm not a happy, peaceful transition to democracy but ungovernability, instability, and dysfunction. We may need to deal with the norm and reality of instability and disorder, rather than a model and an expectation of a more-or-less peaceful, successful transformation to representative, liberal, pluralist government.

These, after all, are countries that are not fully modern or developed, that show many characteristics of other middle-level and transitional regimes. On most socioeconomic indices they rank with Argentina, Brazil, Mexico, and other middle-ranked countries. True, Russia is remarkably advanced in its space and military technologies, but in other areas it bears a closer resemblance to the Third World. There are different levels in Eastern Europe but some countries there are also quite poor. It may be, therefore, that a successful transition to democracy may not occur; rather chaos and disorder will set in. Argentina of the 1930s to 1970s may be the model, not Spain. That is, a model not necessarily of a successful transition to democracy but of a chaotic, disorganized, fragmented, politically polarized country on a *long-term* basis. Maybe that's the kind of model and expectations that we ought to keep in mind for some of the Eastern European states and maybe Russia, rather than the happy, almost antiseptically peaceful transformation to a liberal democratic outcome, which we might prefer. That is a more dismal scenario but it may prove to be a more realistic one.

Chapter 8

Conclusion: Democracy in Iberia, the Latin American Connection, and an Iberic–Latin American Model of Development?

We are now in a position to answer the large questions posed in the Introduction to this book. These are: (1) Are we now witnessing a new Spain and a new Portugal, countries that are fundamentally different from those familiar to us in the (before the mid-1970s) past? (2) How complete and/or consolidated are Spain's and Portugal's transitions to democracy? (3) With all the changes that have occurred, are there continuities with the past as well (and, if so, how powerful) to which we need to pay attention? (4) How extensive have the new international relations between Iberia and Latin America become? And (5) Is there a distinct Iberic-Latin American model of development and, if so, what does it consist of, how does it differ from other models, and what are the possibilities of its being implemented in Iberia or Latin America? Answers to these questions derive from the substantive chapters of this book as well as the materials provided in the companion volume *Democracy and Its Discontents,* and from the author's own ongoing research and field work in Spain and Portugal.

A New Spain, A New Portugal?

To the first question of whether a new Spain and a new Portugal have emerged in the period since the Portuguese revolution in 1974 and the death of Franco in 1975, the answer is, definitively, *yes.* Persons who knew Spain and Portugal in the 1950s and 1960s as poor, "sleepy," rural, agrarian, illiterate, semi-feudal, closed, overwhelmingly Catholic, underdeveloped, authoritarian societies would hardly recognize these two countries today. Moreover, the changes of the past several decades in both countries are deep and profound; these are not just superficial changes. Indeed, one could make the case that *in few countries in the world* have the changes of the past twenty to thirty years been as deep and far-reaching within a short period of time as in Spain and Portugal.

The major areas of change may be enumerated and described briefly under the following headings: cultural, economic, social, political, and international.

1. **Cultural.** A flowering of culture of all kinds has occurred in both countries (especially Spain). But more than that, there have also been profound changes in the political culture, away from a closed, inward-looking, elitist, authoritarian political culture to one that is far more open, free, outward, European-oriented, and democratic.[1]

2. **Economic.** Spain and Portugal, since the 1950s (while Franco and Salazar were still in power), have moved away from their closed, autarchic, statist, and neo-mercantilist policies toward more capitalistic, open, and expansionist economies. They have also, within this forty-year period, gone from being predominantly agricultural, subsistence, and primary product-producing economies to being urban, industrial, manufacturing, and service-based economies; Spain has developed as the ninth or tenth largest economy (in GNP) in the world. Thanks both to these policy changes and the rich European subsidies since they joined the European Economic Community in 1986, per capita income in both Spain and Portugal has vastly increased, reaching about two-thirds the overall Western European averages—although with Portugal still lagging considerably behind Spain.[2]

3. **Social.** Stimulated by the value and economic changes described above, society and social structure in Spain and Portugal have also changed profoundly. The changes include a shift from a predominantly rural to a predominantly urban society, from a condition of widespread illiteracy to one of literacy, from agrarian to industrial, from poverty to far greater affluence, from relatively low life expectancy to essentially European levels. Both countries now have a large and diverse middle class, a new European-oriented entrepreneurial class (as distinct from the older ruling elites), many more professionals and *técnicos*, and a larger and more mature trade union movement. The older two-class society has given way, within certain limits to be spelled out below, to far greater diversity and pluralism. In addition, societal values have changed: toward greater openness and freedom for

women, young people, etc. With these changes have also come drugs, crime, challenges to the traditional family, and divorce—changes Spaniards and Portuguese lament while also taking perverse pride in them as a sign of "modernity."[3]

4. **Political.** Stimulated by the cultural and socioeconomic changes described above, which began in the 1950s and 1960s when Franco and Salazar were still in power, Spain and Portugal also underwent a political transformation to democracy beginning in the mid-1970s. Both countries are, by now, established, self-confident, European parliamentary democracies with the full gamut of democratic institutions: constitution, rule of law, parliament, political parties, regular and competitive elections, informed public opinion, etc. It would be unthinkable, to say nothing of costly in terms of the withdrawal of EEC subsidies and strong international sanctions, for either country to revert to a system of government other than democracy. Over the past two decades democratic institutions and habits have been strongly consolidated.

Although I do not wish to be deterministic about it and though the sequence can and does occur differently in other countries, it is striking that a *successful* democracy in Spain and Portugal (as distinct from earlier unsuccessful efforts) came only *after* both countries had fundamentally altered their political culture and achieved a certain level of socioeconomic development. One is reminded of the reported response of Laureano López Rodó, one of Franco's ablest ministers and a principal architect of Spain's 1960s economic modernization, when he was asked when Spain would achieve democracy. "Only when the per capita income reaches $2,000," was the response. Well, it *was* precisely in the 1970s when Spain's per capita income hit $2,000 that the transition to democracy occurred. Since then, Spain's per capita income has continued to rise, often spectacularly, which helps explain (although it is not the only explanation) why Spain's new democratic institutions seem stronger and more secure than those of Portugal, and why both the now more affluent Iberian democracies are stronger and more secure than those of many of the Latin American nations—more on these themes to follow.

5. **International.** While immense changes have occurred in Spain's and Portugal's domestic situation—culturally, economically, socially, politically—since the mid-1970s, their international activities have expanded enormously as well—particularly Spain's. Under Franco and Salazar, although integrated into NATO and the U.S. defense perimeter, Spain and Portugal remained outcasts from Europe, pariah states, because of their persistent "fascist" regimes. But with the Portuguese Revolution in 1974 and Franco's death the following year—and with continued progress toward

democracy in both countries—Europe not only welcomed the two Iberian countries into its arms but, through subsidies, political and diplomatic assistance, and massive economic aid, assisted in the process. This assistance, the fact of democratic legitimacy, and Spain's and Portugal's own foreign policy ambitions enabled them to break out of their historic isolation and play a larger, more ambitious foreign policy role. Spain sought to play a leadership role in Europe, Latin America, the Middle East, and *vis-à-vis* the United States; Portugal, although a smaller country and more preoccupied for a longer time with its domestic political situation, also came to play a larger role in Europe, in Ibero-American affairs, and in Southern Africa. Along with the domestic changes, these new energies in foreign policy signaled that Spain and Portugal had become "normal" nations, no longer "exotic" or "different," no longer outcasts or nations with large inferiority complexes, but welcome and acceptable members of the family of democratic nations and ready again to play a commensurately larger international role.

In addition, both countries are now also far more integrated into global economic trends than ever before. Breaking out of their traditional autarchic mold, both Spain and Portugal have welcomed foreign investment, modernized their industries, joined the EEC and GATT, and become competitive in global markets. They have opened up their markets to foreign competition and, in turn, have themselves become players at a global economic level. Along with this opening to world trade and competition has also come global social trends; rock music, blue jeans, Coca-Cola, consumerism, and—not least—the desire for democracy and freedom.

Transitions to Democracy: How Complete?

The second major question posed in the Introduction is: How *complete* are the transitions to democracy in Spain and Portugal?

First, let us acknowledge, as described above, the major accomplishments that Spain and Portugal have made in the past twenty years, including toward democracy. As a result, most of the literature on the transitions has been celebratory—and, for the most part, with reason. But while we celebrate Iberia's evolution toward democracy, that should not blind us to the warts and problems that remain or the incompleteness of the process itself.

And that is the second point that needs to be made: that the transition to democracy is a process, a journey, and that it is *always* incomplete for *all* countries. Hence, it does not to me seem appropriate to ask whether Spain and Portugal have *completed* the process as yet. Nor is it satisfactory to elevate short-term evaluative criteria as markers to indicate the country has satisfactorily passed the test: for example, the often used criteria of *two* successful shifts, by electoral means, from one administration to the next (by this criterion Portugal would pass but not Spain—at least until the PSOE government yields peacefully to an elected successor). Instead of viewing democracy as an either-or proposition or with clear and definite markers on a well-traveled route to democracy, we need to envision the process as a continuum, a spectrum running from authoritarianism to democracy—with countries strung out at various points along the line. At the same time, we need to recognize that, depending on internal events, countries can replace each other and move up or down along the continuum.

To make an evaluation of where a country fits on this continuum, some clear criteria need to be employed. The clearest and most widely used criteria are institutional: regular, honest, competitive elections; constitutionalism, the rule of law, civil liberties; and pluralism and free competition among interest groups. But I wish to add to this list the criterion of a democratic political culture (egalitarianism, diversity of opinions and respect for them, civility in dealing with views and people who may be different from one's own), and I am willing to incorporate some level of socioeconomic criteria as well as a necessary base for democracy: literacy, per capita income, social programs, how equitably wealth is distributed, standard of living, and quality of life. It is possible to develop measures or indices for rank-ordering countries on each of these criteria.

We need not do that entire exercise here to recognize that, by these criteria, some countries are more democratic than others. While we are all happy about the democratic progress that Spain and Portugal have made, for example, the question I am asking is whether they are, in terms of the authoritarianism-democracy continuum suggested above, as yet as democratic as other acknowledged, long-term democracies. As democratic as Great Britain, for example, or Holland, or Denmark, or Switzerland? How does Iberian democracy compare with the United States, with Canada? How about a comparison with other, more recent democracies such as Germany or Italy? How about the country—Greece—that returned to democracy at the same time, in the mid-1970s, that Spain and Portugal did? Or how about the more recent transitions (hopefully) to democracy in Russia and Eastern Europe? Even without working out all the exact measures and comparisons, it is probably safe to say that most of us think of Spain and Portugal as perhaps not quite as safely and securely democratic as most of Western Europe or North America, probably about the same as Greece, and more democratic than Russia or Eastern Europe.

Continuing with the idea of a continuum, let us now bring in Latin America. Clearly, democracy in Spain and Portugal is stabler and better institutionalized—and has a stronger base—than is that of Guatemala, Bolivia, Haiti, or other of the less institutionalized, less developed countries of Latin America. But what about Argentina, Colombia, or Venezuela, which not only are well-institutionalized and democracies but also, some time ago, passed that magic threshold of having a per capita income of $2,000 per year identified by López Rodó as providing the necessary socioeconomic base for democracy? Or how about Chile, Costa Rica, or Uruguay, all of which have longer if not stronger democratic traditions than either Spain or Portugal? Another suggestion might be to disaggregate Spain and Portugal, to treat them separately since they are, in fact, at different levels themselves. Even in these lights, my own assessment would be that Spain probably outranks *all* the Latin American countries (but is not yet as democratic as most of the rest of Western Europe) in terms of the stability and level of consolidation of its democracy. Portugal, in contrast, which has a far lower per capita income than Spain and is less well institutionalized, may be grouped in my view with the more advanced Latin American democracies—let us say with Chile, Uruguay, and Argentina. In these countries, democracy is probably consolidated but there may still be challenges to it.

Hence, we return to the formulation in the introductory chapter: that Spain is not only but two-thirds of the way to Western Europe's level of social and economic development but that it is still only about 70 percent of the way—to put a number on it—to democracy as well. For Portugal I would put the figure at 60 percent, slightly below that of Spain but about at the same level as the most advanced Latin American countries. In these ways not only can we usefully compare Spain and Portugal to Europe but we can also bring in a comparison—and an extension of our continuum—to Latin America as well. To complete the comparisons mentioned so far, while Spain and Portugal are, respectively, 70 percent and 60 percent of the way to democracy, Russia may be only 40 percent of the way there and Eastern Europe (ranging from Bulgaria, Romania, and the former Yugoslavia in the south to Poland, Slovakia, and the Czech Republic in the north) ranges between 30 and 50 percent.

We (and others) have spoken at length of the remarkable successes in Spain's and Portugal's transitions to democracy, but scholars have paid less attention to the weaknesses and problem areas. Why is it, in other words, that we rate Spain and Portugal only two-thirds of the way to the European democratic model and not all of the way?

Let us consider the weaknesses of Portuguese democracy first. To begin, Portugal remains a poor and underdeveloped country in many respects, with high rates of illiteracy, inadequate social programs, an unconsolidated and often fragmented middle class, and vast social gaps between rich and poor. In other words, the social and economic basis for Portuguese democracy remains precarious. Second, public opinion in Portugal is often ill-informed and ill-heeded; public opinion is seldom consulted or listened to in what is still, often, an elite-directed democracy. Moreover, the public opinion surveys we have often reflect disturbing preferences: for the order and stability of Salazar, or for the order with *some* freedom of Caetano; at the same time these surveys register significant disgust for the current democratic institutions: political parties and parliament.[4] A third and related factor is the continuing weakness and ineffectiveness of democratic political institutions including the parties, the ministries, public administration, interest organizations, parliament, and the offices of president and prime minister. Portugal's semi-presidential system, for example, is itself a reflection of the country's still transitional nature, as distinct from a fully consolidated democracy.[5]

There are also, fourth, weaknesses in the implementation of policy programs: too much inefficiency, patronage, and "private regardingness"—as distinct from "public regardingness," a concern for genuinely public-oriented programs. In addition—and because of the previously listed factors— considerable disillusionment with democracy has set in, as evidenced in public apathy, declining voter turnout, widespread disenchantment with *all* the political parties and candidates, and significantly high levels of preferences for the order, discipline, and austerity of the old (Salazar-Caetano) regime. These factors, especially when combined, make me conclude that while Portugal has made a successful transition and is a more-or-less consolidated democracy, it remains an imperfect democracy, a democracy with many problems, with severe gaps. As one of Portugal's leading young scholars put it, the *only* chapter in Portugal's journey to democracy that has been closed at this time is the civil-military relations one where in fact full civilian control has been achieved.[6] Portugal seems to me—rather like Argentina, Chile, or Uruguay—safely in the democratic camp but the warts are such that democracy cannot be taken for granted or its severe problems ignored.

What about Spain?[7] First, Spain's social and economic base remains much stronger than that of Portugal and thus provides a stronger foundation for democracy—although the exceedingly high Spanish unemployment rate (over 20 percent, the highest in Western Europe) is very worrisome. Second, despite Spain's disillusionment with Prime Minister Felipe González and the Socialist Party, despite corruption, scandal, patrimonialism, and a certain weariness with partisan politics, Spain maintains an apparently unshakable attachment to democratic values. Third, many of Spain's political institutions—rather like Portugal's—remain weak: the political parties have severe leadership and organizational problems, the Senate has yet to discover a set

of functions, parliament is often chaotic and disorganized, the prime minister's office is beset by scandal, and political associations are weak in both
numbers and influence. In addition, both Spanish unions and the parties are
still heavily subsidized by the state, a situation that bears a striking resemblance to earlier corporatism (more on this below) *and*, given Spain's
mounting economic troubles, cannot be maintained indefinitely.

A fourth area of concern is in the realm of public policy. Because of
generous European subsidies during the past decade, Spain has not yet had
to face the wrenching pressures of state downsizing, austerity, and privatization that most other countries have. Instead, with these subsidies, Spain was
able to put in place an exceedingly elaborate and generous welfare program,
which the country can no longer afford. Particularly as the subsidies start
running out in 1997, Spain will have to face a radical and painful cutting
back of both social programs and of the oversized, even bloated, Spanish
state, which since Franco's death has become a huge patronage agency whose
political and economic plums are crucial to the political survival of the
Spanish government. When I was in Spain for the 1993 parliamentary
election, it was significant—particularly after having just come from an
extended research trip to South America, where austerity and privatization
constituted virtually the only agenda—that neither of Spain's major political
parties said a word about state downsizing. Now the Popular Party (PP) is
beginning to talk about it, although certainly not in detail, even though
everyone now recognizes that belt-tightening adjustments are necessary.

There are other problems as well. Spain is becoming—again—a more
conflictual society. Parties, institutions, and associational life in general are
still often fragile and not well developed. There are severe—and growing—
financial woes. Corruption, nepotism, and patrimonialism are growing in
the public sphere, reaching levels, as some critics have put it, "comparable
to Mexico's"—which is a truly devastating critique. There is a certain
disillusionment with democracy as failing to deliver as much as promised,
which is reflected in growing cynicism, political apathy, and declining voter
turnout. And yet, almost no Spaniard wants to contemplate, let alone favor,
democracy's alternatives; and despite the problems there still is, as Ramón
Arango puts it, that "unshakable attachment to democratic values."[8]

The question for both Portugal and Spain is: Are these just the normal
problems of a normal democracy? Or are the problems deeper than that? The
answer is, both: these are the normal problems of a new and emerging
democracy, *and* there are some deeper issues involved.

The Question of Continuities

While we all acknowledge that the changes in Spain and Portugal over the past twenty years have been immense, there are also important continuities. The continuities are more difficult to discuss without emotion in large part because Spaniards and Portuguese—and frequently the scholars who study both countries—would prefer to emphasize the changes. Given that the past in Spain and Portugal (Franco, Salazar, authoritarianism, dictatorship) has often been painful, Spain and Portugal would generally prefer not to be reminded of it. They much prefer the recent accomplishments—transitions to democracy, social change, freedom, new welfare programs—over the heavy and still often present hand of history. This is an understandable preference but not one that serious scholars should also countenance. The fact is, there are many continuities in Spain and Portugal that reach back before the major changes of the mid-1970s and that continue to the present.

Political Culture

Spain and Portugal have democratized enormously since the mid-1970s; no one would deny the changes. Yet in my research on these two countries, I am struck by the continuities as well of a variety of historic traits and practices that continue to coexist alongside the newer democratic values. There is still a lot of authoritarianism in Spain and Portugal, in social and class relations as well as in the political realm. There is still a great deal of elitism, of centralized and top-down attitudes, of *dirigisme* in both the economic and political spheres. Spaniards and Portuguese still tend to look to the state for guidance, direction, and economic opportunities, which helps give rise to corruption, patrimonialism, and corporatism. A number of these traits have been reduced since the mid-1970s but they have by no means been entirely eliminated—as witness the widespread criticisms for these practices of the recent regimes of both Felipe González and Aníbal Cavaco Silva.

The issue of continuity is made more complex by the fact that even within the formal structures of Spanish and Portuguese democracy, many informal and not-so-democratic practices from the past remain. Spanish and Portuguese democracy, for example, still tends to be organic, unified, centralized, integralist, corporatist, and Rousseauean democracy; it is not the unfettered pluralist democracy of Locke, Jefferson, or Madison. Spanish and Portuguese democracy is still shot through with family favoritism, nepotism, patronage, and patrimonialism; in corporatist fashion, various groups try to capture and hive off for themselves whole areas of public policy. Attitudes within the public bureaucracies of both countries are still often haughty and elitist; these are not always agencies designed to be responsible and to serve the public. Private regardingness too often triumphs over public regardingness, even under democracy. The formal structures of Spain and Portugal are clearly democratic but private practice and procedures too often fall short of that.

Class and Social Structure

Democracy implies more than institutions; it also means certain levels of egalitarianism, civic responsibility, and mutual respect among the classes. Both Spain and Portugal have changed in these aspects but in quite different ways.

In Portugal, once the initial revolution occurred in 1974 that overthrew Caetano and the *Estado Novo*, a "second revolution" took place that reached deeper into society. The old elites lost power, often saw their property taken over, and many had to flee the country. At the same time, many other hierarchies and systems of authority were similarly upset: children rebelled against parents, peasants against landlords, maids against *madames*, workers against employers, lower military ranks against senior, hospital staff against doctors, and so on. The Portuguese revolution of the mid-1970s had aspects of a genuine social revolution.

But since then, many reversals have occurred. Most of the old elite is now back in Portugal, many have recovered their earlier confiscated properties, some have been elected to political office. Meanwhile, the more traditional, conservative, Catholic political culture that is historic Portugal has also, in many areas of national life, reasserted itself. At the same time, the system of authoritarian social and political relations, the numerous hierarchies, the system of rank orders, the "society of uniforms" that I wrote about in my mid-1970s book on Portugal,[9] have all made a comeback. So Portugal remains a dual society of class and political relations that is egalitarian and democratic at many levels but authoritarian, elitist, and hierarchical at others.

Spain's transition was less dramatic than Portugal's but may have been more profound. First, Spain did not have a social revolution in the mid-1970s when Franco died, as Portugal did when Caetano was ousted. There was no violent or wholesale ouster of the old elites, no dramatic class shifts, no broad upsetting of existing hierarchies. But second, Spain's social relations did go through a long, *evolutionary* process of change that may have reached deeper than Portugal's quick but perhaps shallower and less long-lasting changes. The profound generational, cultural, and social changes that shaped a new Spain began in the 1960s; when Franco died in 1975 the society beneath him had already been altered so fundamentally that it was no longer the society of the past. Here we are talking about such social arenas as children in relation to parents, the family structure, the role of women (often working and more independent), the efficient and egalitarian attitudes of clerks in department stores, and a host of other social relations. In this sense I find Spain a more egalitarian and, therefore, more democratic society than Portugal.

But these changes are more apparent in Spain's larger cities than they are in small towns and the countryside. Moreover, there are many areas of Spanish national life—industry, banking, many government ministries, the judiciary, armed forces, social life and class relations—where the older hierarchies and sense of place and position are still powerfully present. These hierarchies and the elitism that goes with them did not have to face revolutionary upheaval as in Portugal, and many areas of Spanish life were able to insulate themselves in part from the large cultural trends occurring and to preserve their older ways of operating. My own personal research, travel, and living experience in all these countries leads me to conclude that Spain is a less egalitarian and, hence, less democratic country than some others in Europe where I have also done extensive research: Holland, Austria, and Switzerland, for example. Then too, it is striking that the austerity and belt-tightening program carried out by the Spanish *Socialist* Party in the 1980s and 1990s has *consistently* hit hardest at the working class and that the party leadership, caught up in corruption, nepotism, and high living, has become increasingly estranged from the Spanish working class. The corrupt, inexcusable behavior of the PSOE in office has led more and more Spaniards (and not just a single, "ornery" American political scientist—me) to question just how much has really changed in Spanish class relations and political behavior.[10]

The State

Another area of continuity in both Spain and Portugal is the state. Here we are talking not just about the large size of the state but about political attitudes as well in these two countries where people continue to look to the state as the source of all jobs, goods, contracts, favors, welfare, monopolies, and special privileges.

I spend a considerable portion of my time in Latin America where, in the past decade, a veritable revolution has taken place in terms of the downsizing, privatizing, and streamlining of the state. Some of this reduction in the size of the Latin American state has come from U.S. pressure, some from World Bank and International Monetary Fund pressure, and some from Latin America's own realization, in their new post–Cold War, international, interdependent, and intensely competitive environment, of the need for greater rationality and efficiency in the operation of the state sector. The causes are not so important as the *fact* that the Latin American states, which grow out of the same strong statist or *dirigeste* tradition as the Iberian states, are now leaner and more efficient that they were previously. Therefore, it is a considerable shock to me when I go to Spain and Portugal to discover that their big, bloated, inefficient, patronage-dominated states are still in place, that these two countries have been able largely to avoid what in fact has now become a global, neoliberal trend to reduce the size and make the state more efficient.

The chief cause, we have seen, for avoiding this issue in Spain and Portugal is all those European subsidies over the past decade. The flow of financial resources and aid from the EEC since Spain and Portugal joined the community in 1986 has been immense. These subsidies have enabled Spain and Portugal to avoid even talking about the politically sensitive topic of austerity and reducing state size, let alone doing anything about them. The result is that Spain and Portugal have among the most bloated and inefficient state sectors in all of Europe. The sheer size and extent of public bureaucracy and the vast patronage resources available are the single most important cause in explaining the truly mind-numbing corruption, especially in Spain, that has set in.

Even worse, the Spanish and Portuguese state systems, living on rich subsidies and not having to downsize, are often woefully inefficient and hence unable to compete in a far more contentious global marketplace, which they must be able to do once the subsidies end. Almost alone among countries in the world, Spain and Portugal have not had to undergo the Thatcher-Reagan-like reforms that will make their economies more productive, more efficient, and more competitive. Moreover, the size and vast resources available through the state have perpetuated the habit of looking to the state, rather than to one's own initiatives, for handouts, patronage, and special favors. One understands the need that both Europe and Spain and Portugal saw in earlier decades to prop up their economies as a way of binding them into Europe and to democracy; but these same policies in this new, post–Cold War, intensely competitive, global marketplace may well turn out to be disastrous in long-range terms.

Corporatism

As we know from the Comparative Politics literature,[11] strong states and the corporative organization of societal and interest groups often go together.

Not only have Spain and Portugal maintained strong state systems but they also continue to practice new forms of corporatism.

Spain and Portugal have long histories of what we have termed natural, traditional, or medieval corporatism. Then in the 1930s under Franco and Salazar, both countries, facing economic and political crises, adopted a set of manifest corporatist institutions. These corporatist institutions were repudiated in the Portuguese revolution of 1974 and with Franco's death in 1975. But the formal outlawing of corporatism did not mean that the informal practice of corporatism was discontinued. In fact, in both countries corporatism remains very much present, usually unacknowledged, in new forms, but present nonetheless. I call this "everyday corporatism": the continuing efforts, even today and within the structure of an architecturally democratic state, of virtually every group—labor, business, military, farmers, bureaucrats, retirees, journalists, bankers, film producers, regional and local governments, state-owned enterprises, etc.—to extract and/or protect its special contract, license, monopoly, patronage position, and financial subsidy or entitlements from the state.

Portugal and Spain have moved from the older form of state corporatism to a new form, or neocorporatism. Actually, given the vast size and power of the Spanish and Portuguese state sector, it is often state corporatism that continues to be practiced. The state negotiates pacts between labor and capital to provide for "social peace." It is still often the state, and not the marketplace, that determines wages, production, and prices. These are the hallmarks of state corporatism—still often present in Spain and Portugal. But on top of this older, more authoritarian state corporatism has come a newer, social-welfare-based system of neocorporatism in which lower-class groups are often brought into (and coopted by) the bureaucratic state system. It is not hard to see why corporatism and a vast, patronage-dominated state system go hand in hand.

But because of the earlier experiences under Franco and Salazar when corporatism was largely discredited, it is hard for Spain and Portugal to admit that they still practice corporatism. The term is seldom used in either country because of its political connotations, and, unlike many other countries, there is little use of the now well-known corporatist analytical framework by Spanish or Portuguese scholars. Nevertheless corporatism is an important continuity in Spanish and Portuguese social and political life whether they wish to acknowledge it or not. Moreover, both the political culture and the perpetuation of a strong statist tradition guarantee that corporatism, in one form or another, will be present in Iberia for a long time to come.

Iberia and Latin America

In the mid-1980s, with significant Tinker Foundation support, we undertook a collaborative effort to explore Spain's and Portugal's foreign policy in

Latin America.[12] This was a major project involving leading academic scholars as well as policy-makers, and exploring all aspects of Spanish/ Portuguese foreign policy in Latin America: cultural, political, diplomatic, economic, strategic. We had all been impressed, especially by Spain's more aggressive, expansive, and vigorous post-Franco foreign policy in Latin America. But at the end of our investigations, based on Spain's continued economic, diplomatic, and institutional debilities, our conclusion was that Spain would not become a major player in Latin America, that it would certainly not challenge U.S. dominance in the hemisphere, and that Portugal would continue to play only a limited role.

The main conclusions of that study still stand. On the other hand, Spain has continued to play a more aggressive and expansive role in Latin America than we had expected ten years ago. Not only has Spain expanded its cultural and diplomatic activities in Latin America but it has put real meat on these bones by increasing its trade and investments as well. Spain has not only aggressively pursued a vigorous investment strategy in the Spanish-speaking countries—to be expected—but it has now become a major investor in Portuguese-speaking Brazil as well. In addition, Spain has pledged some twenty billion dollars in aid to Latin America as part of the Fifth Centenary of Columbus's discovery of America in 1492. The *Quincentenario* also served as a stimulus to Spain's larger goal of forming an Interamerican Community of Nations whose heads of state now meet on a yearly basis. Not only is the United States excluded from this "Hispanic Commonwealth" but the community has also staked out foreign policy positions—most prominently on Cuba—either independent of or contrary to U.S. policy. Spain has also used its position in the EEC to build up both a greater European—and especially Spain's own—presence in Latin America. Meanwhile, Portugal, after years of preoccupation with its own domestic politics, has returned to playing a greater foreign policy role, both in Southern Africa where Portugal has a long history *and* in Latin America. Especially for Spain, Latin America occupies a place in its foreign policy second only to Europe.[13]

But Spain's influence in Latin America has been exercised not only in these concrete economic, political, and diplomatic ways. Spain, and to a lesser extent smaller, poorer, weaker Portugal, has also tried to present itself as a model for Latin America. But the question is, a model of what? It is to this issue of a distinct, unique, Iberic-Latin model of development—and what that model would consist of—that we turn next.

An Iberic-Latin Model of Development?

I once held out hope, about twenty years ago, that Iberia and Latin America would develop their own distinctive model of development.[14] A number of the traits—corporatism, organic statism, bureaucratic politics, an updated patrimonialism and mercantilism, a balance between central state authority and group autonomy, others—that would go into such a model were specified. But several of these traits were apparently too closely associated with the "corporatist" and "bureaucratic authoritarianism" regimes of the 1970s. Not only were they sometimes discredited for that reason but, when Iberia and Latin America began to move toward democracy in the mid-to-late-1970s, the model seemed to some to have been superseded as well.

Even as Latin America and Iberia moved toward democracy, however, I continued to argue that the form that democracy took—reflecting these earlier political cultural and sociopolitical traditions—would continue to exhibit unique features.[15] The form would be Rousseauian rather than Jeffersonian democracy: still centralized, organic, bureaucratic, statist, and with many "natural" corporatist features. I suggested that the historic dynamic tension in state-society relations—between an authoritarian and top-down state and the effort of functional society units (Church, armed forces, business, labor, etc.) to maintain their autonomy—would tip, now (but not completely) toward the societal side and that this would be called "democracy." In my research I was especially interested in the Spanish case, which, with the rewriting of the constitution in 1977 and the dynamic and ongoing renegotiation between the state and its component corporate units *and* between the central government and the regions, seemed to be arriving both at a unique, *Spanish* model of parliamentary democracy *and* providing a model from which Latin America could learn.[16]

But the idea of a distinctive, updated, now democratic Iberic–Latin American model of development, regardless of its accuracy, never developed the enthusiasm I had thought it would. For one thing, Spain and Portugal, after the long shadow of Franco and Salazar who had emphasized their countries' uniqueness often in inappropriate and repressive ways, no longer wanted to be considered "distinctive" or "different"; they wanted instead to emphasize their Europeanness and their conformity to European ways. Second, in both U.S. academic and Washington policy circles, the notion was widespread that democracy and human rights were one and universal: the model was the United States or perhaps Western Europe, everyone else had to live up to our own ethnocentric standards, and there was little understanding of, room for, or sympathy toward a more pluralistic, culturally conditioned understanding of democracy. And third, the Latin Americans were not much in favor of a distinct model of development: either they resented Spain's efforts, condescendingly, to serve as a model for them; or they distrusted the implications of an indigenous model (which would have to include elements of authoritarianism and corporatism which they, like Spain and Portugal, wanted to forget); or they wished to be in the forefront of "advanced" democracy (social democracy) rather than facing the harder task of building a democracy true to their own traditions.[17]

The result was that the idea of an indigenous, home-grown model of democracy for both Iberia and Latin America languished. Spain has failed to build on the several elements (unique patterns of state-society relations, regionalism) of its own transition to democracy that were truly distinctive. And Latin America, in its eagerness to be accepted by the rest of the developed and democratic world, has chosen to try to ignore what is distinctive in its own culture and history in order to emulate the West. The result is that Spain is—and takes pride in being—"just another" normal, "boring," European parliamentary democracy. Spain and Portugal have consciously, purposely, chosen to ape and imitate European ways, and to downplay those parts of their political culture that are distinctively Spanish or Portuguese. Latin America, meantime, clings to an ideal-type model of democracy largely fashioned in the United States, while blotting out or suppressing those traditions from its past that are often not particularly democratic.

It remains unclear how long this situation can go on. Spain and Portugal can probably continue indefinitely as European-style democracies. Their democratic institutions are quite solidly in place and no attractive alternative seems likely to emerge any time soon. In the cases of the Iberian democracies, it seems to me unfortunate that they have chosen not to emphasize the features that make them distinctive or to take pride in a form of democracy that combines indigenous elements with universal norms. But that is their decision and I understand the political motives (desiring to be *fully* European after so many centuries on the periphery) behind it. Spain's and Portugal's reluctance to acknowledge and deal more realistically with their own historic ways of doing things may be lamentable but it is certainly not fatal, so far as the survival of Iberian democracy goes.

But in Latin America, I am not so sure. The Latin American countries are, in general, far less economically and socially developed than are Spain and Portugal; their newly democratic political institutions are considerably less consolidated than those in the Iberian Peninsula; and Latin America lacks anything comparable to the subsidies and "protection" afforded to Spain and Portugal by the European Community. Latin America has adopted a model of democracy largely imported from abroad but without adequately adapting it to local realities. That model can probably survive as long as the times are prosperous and the United States continues to oversee the situation like a mother hen watching her brood. But economic prosperity remains very tenuous as the Mexican *peso* crisis of 1994–95 made clear, and U.S. policy toward the region is notoriously fickle. Should Latin America enter into troubled economic times coupled with disinterest or benign neglect on the part of the United States, then its mainly imported democratic political institutions could quickly find themselves in very serious trouble. Already in Argentina, Chile, Peru, Mexico, Haiti, the Dominican Republic, and *many* other countries, serious but still largely unacknowledged compromises have had to be made between the democratic ideals enshrined in the laws and constitutions *and* the actual, operating realities that stem from the fact that these countries often have other traditions that are not fully democratic.[18]

Eventually these operating realities of Latin America will have to be acknowledged and dealt with realistically. They cannot be simply denied or wished away. Latin American politics is often a mixture, a hodgepodge, a crazy-quilt of democratic and not-so-democratic practices. We need to recognize this fact and not, in our enthusiasm for such pure and pristine models of democracy that they don't even apply in the United States or Western Europe, engage in unrealistic wishful thinking. Why cannot we acknowledge that Latin America—and to some, but lesser, extent Spain and Portugal as well—has both a liberal-republican-democratic tradition and set of institutions, *and* a set that still exhibits many authoritarian, elitist, organic-statist, patrimonialist, and corporatist features? And could we not design a constitution and institutional framework that not only reflects these realities but is also stabler and more functional for being so? And wouldn't this kind of realism and the stability and functionality that would flow from it best serve not only Iberian and Latin American goals but also U.S. policy goals in both regions?

Could we not design a system, then, that combined both democratic and statist features? That dealt realistically, as in the 1977 Spanish constitution, with the need for centralized decision-making but decentralized implementation? That combined Rousseauian idealism with the more prosaic features of Lockean electoral politics? That came to grips realistically with the need for a new, updated form of corporatism rather than simply dismissing and sweeping corporatism under the rug? That better balanced human rights with the need for stability and order? That combined the new but untried neoliberalism with the practical realities of statism? Such a system would have to be further adapted to the distinct realities of each country. Moreover, it would have to be a system that provides for dynamic change since, while we need realistically to balance both democratic and statist features, for example, we also want to encourage movement toward a more democratic direction.

I believe it would be possible to fashion such a more balanced system that, at the same time, reflects Iberian and Latin American realities and uniqueness. I believe such a system would be useful and helpful to the countries involved *and* to U.S. policy, which is too often based on hypocritical notions that hold Latin American countries up to democratic standards that the United States itself fails to practice. But such a more creative and nuanced policy may be too complicated for the United States to understand and carry out, and it is understandable why the Iberian and Latin American nations are reluctant to undertake it. On the other hand, a politics that emphasized indigenous as well as imported solutions *would* give Spain a true leadership role in Latin America and in much of the Third World, and it would give Latin America the opportunity—really for the first time—to wrestle realistically with its own fused, mixed, and overlapping traditions.

Notes

1. See Chapter 4, as well as Richard Gunther, *Politics and Culture in Spain* (Ann Arbor: University of Michigan, Institute for Social Research, 1988); and Gunther (ed.), *Politics, Society, and Democracy: The Case of Spain* (Boulder, Colo.: Westview Press, 1993).

2. The best source is Erik N. Baklanoff, who has written extensively on these themes; his most recent study is "Spain's Economic Strategy toward the 'Nations of its Historical Community: The Reconquest' of Latin America," *Journal of Interamerican Studies and World Affairs*, 38 (Spring, 1996) 105–128.

3. An excellent survey is John Hooper, *The Spaniards: A Portrait of the New Spain* (London: Penguin, 1986).

4. The best source is Mario Bacalhão, *Atitudes, Opiniões e Comportamentos Políticos dos Portugueses: 1973–1993* (Lisbon: Fundação Luso Americano Para o Desenvolvimento, 1995).

5. See, for example, Maritheresa Frain, "Presidential-Prime Ministerial Relations in Portugal: Soares and Cavaco-Silva, 1985–95." Paper presented at the Sixth International Meeting of the International Conference Group on Portugal, University of New Hampshire, Durham (September 28–October 1, 1995); also David Corkill, "The Political System and the Consolidation of Democracy in Portugal," *Parliamentary Affairs* 46 (October 1993), 517–33.

6. Antonio Costa Pinto, "Evaluating the Transition to Democracy." Presentation at the Conference on "Twenty Years of Iberian Democracy: An Assessment," Minda de Gunzberg Center for European Studies, Harvard University, Cambridge, Mass., April 7–9, 1995.

7. Based on the author's research in Spain as well as the papers and presentations at the Conference on "Twenty Years of Iberian Democracy: An Assessment"; also Richard Gillespie, "The Continuing Debate on Democratisation in Spain," *Parliamentary Affairs* 46 (October 1993), 534–48.

8. Ramón Arango, *Spain: Democracy Regained* (Boulder, Colo.: Westview Press, 1995).

9. Howard J. Wiarda, *Corporatism and Development: The Portuguese Experience* (Amherst: University of Massachusetts Press, 1977).

10. Over the years I have seldom agreed with the interpretations of James Petras but I agree with his findings on Spain; see James Kurth and James Petras (eds.), *Mediterranean Paradoxes: The Politics and Social Structure of Southern Europe* (Oxford, UK: Berg, 1993).

11. See my own new book, *Corporatism and Comparative Politics* (New York: M. E. Sharpe, 1996).

12. Howard J. Wiarda (ed.), *The Iberian–Latin American Connection* (Boulder, Colo.: Westview Press, 1986).

13. Baklanoff, "Spain's Economic Strategy."

14. Howard J. Wiarda, "Toward a Framework for the Study of Political Change in the Iberic–Latin Tradition: The Corporative Model," *World Politics* XXV (January 1973), 206–35; *Corporatism and National Development in Latin America* (Boulder, Colo.: Westview Press, 1981); *Politics and Social Change in Latin America: Still a Distinct Tradition?* 3rd ed. (Boulder, Colo.: Westview Press, 1992); and *Ethnocentrism in Foreign Policy: Can We Understand the Third World?* (Washington, D.C.: American Enterprise Institute for Public Policy Research, 1985).

15. *Politics and Social Change*, especially the Conclusion of the third edition; "The Future of Reform in the Southern Cone: Can Democracy Be Sustained?" *The Washington Quarterly*, 18 (Summer 1995), 91–102; "Historical Determinants of the Latin American State: The Tradition of Bureaucratic-Patrimonialism, Corporatism, Centralism, and Authoritarianism," in Menno Vellinga (ed.), *The Changing Role of the State in Latin America* (Boulder, Colo.: Westview Press, 1996).

16. Howard J. Wiarda, *Politics in Iberia: The Political Systems of Spain and Portugal* (New York: HarperCollins, 1992).

17. I tried to wrestle with the Iberian and Latin American receptions to my corporatism writings in "Interpreting Iberian–Latin American Interrelations: Paradigm Consensus and Conflict" in *The Iberian–Latin American Connection*; and in "Does Europe Still Stop at the Pyrenees or Does Latin America Begin There? Iberia, Latin America, and the Second Enlargement of the European Community" (Washington, D.C.: AEI, Center for Hemispheric Studies, Occasional Papers Series No. 2, 1982).

18. Howard J. Wiarda, "The Cause of Democratic Elections in Latin America: Are We on the Right Track? (Washington, D.C.: Center for Strategic and International Studies, Americas Program, Occasional Papers Series, Summer 1995).

Index

About the Author

Howard J. Wiarda is Leonard J. Horwitiz Professor of Political Science and Latin American Studies at the University of Massachusetts/Amherst, Senior Associate at the Center for Strategic and International Studies (CSIS) in Washington, D.C., and Professor of National Security Studies at the National Defense University in Washington. He is the author or editor of *Democracy and Its Discontents, Latin American Politics, Politics in Iberia, American Foreign Policy,* and *An Introduction to Comparative Politics.* Professor Wiarda's research and writings bridge the fields of comparative politics, Latin America, southern Europe, foreign policy, Russia, and East Asia. A number of his writings have been influential in these academic fields as well as in the Washington foreign policy debate.